JOHN REGISTER:
PERSISTENT OBSERVER

JOHN REGISTER
PERSISTENT OBSERVER

BY BARNABY CONRAD III

SAN JOSE MUSEUM OF ART
WOODFORD PRESS, SAN FRANCISCO

In Loving Memory of John Register

Copyright © 1998 by Barnaby Conrad III

All rights reserved. No part of this book may be reproduced in any form without written permission from the publisher.

Printed in Canada.

Book and cover design:
Tom Morgan, Blue Design, www.bluedes.com

Library of Congress Catalog Card Number 98-61588
ISBN: 0-942627-50-4

Published in collaboration with the San Jose Museum of Art, San Jose, and Modernism Gallery, San Francisco, California.

Distributed in the United States, Canada and Europe by
Andrews McMeel Publishing
4520 Main Street
Kansas City, MO 64111-7701

Woodford Press
660 Market Street
San Francisco, CA 94104

C. David Burgin, Editor and Publisher
Daniel C. Ross, CEO and Publisher

Acknowledgments:

This book and exhibition could not have been produced without the thought, care and perseverance of Katya Kashkooli, Martin Muller, Cathy Register, Peter Register, Josi Callan, Peter Gordon, Patty Hickson, Karen Kienzle, Cathy Kimball and Diane Maxwell, as well as book designer Tom Morgan, editor Richard Defendorf, and publishers Dave Burgin and Dan Ross. I also thank Anthony Weller, Mark Hugh Miller, Dr. Peter Selz, Robert Flynn Johnson, Eugene Beck, John Martin and David Register for their help with the manuscript. My assistant Andrew Nelson, Margaret Jo Feldman and Winston Conrad also were essential. Finally, I offer my gratitude to Cathy Register for believing in this project from start to finish. — B. C. III

The San Jose Museum of Art thanks the following corporate sponsors of the exhibition: Wilson Sonsini Goodrich & Rosati, Bank of America Foundation, Citibank, and 3Com. Additional Support has been provided by the Museum's Council of 100.

Pages 2-3: *Bunker Hill*, 1989, oil on canvas, 35 x 50 inches
Collection of Martin Muller

Page 5: *Gas, Food*, 1993, oil on canvas, 50 x 50 inches
Collection of Bob and Pat Eggers

Pages 6-7: *Watching the Storm (Denver)*, 1988, oil on canvas, 40 x 90 inches
Collection of Barnaby Conrad III

Page 8: *View of Venice Boardwalk*, 1988, oil on canvas, 49 x 49 inches
Collection of Valerie Curtain

Page 11: *Mojave Pool*, 1976, oil on canvas, 35 x 45 inches
Collection of John and Barbara Martin/Black Sparrow Press

CONTENTS

Exhibition Tour Itinerary	10
Foreword by Josi Callan	12
Preface by Dr. Peter Selz	14
John Register: Persistent Observer By Barnaby Conrad III	
Introduction	20
1 - Early Life	24
2 - First Paintings	42
3 - A Sense Of Mortality	64
4 - The Return To The West	84
5 - Late Years	120
6 - Going Towards The Vanishing Point	170
Notes	184
Bibliography	187
Chronology	188
San Jose Museum of Art Trustees and Staff	189
Exhibition Checklist	190
Index	191

JOHN REGISTER: A RETROSPECTIVE
Exhibition Tour Itinerary

San Jose Museum of Art San Jose, California	January 16 - May 9, 1999
Frye Art Museum Seattle, Washington	July 2 - August 29, 1999
Palm Springs Desert Museum Palm Springs, California	September 25 - November 28, 1999
Frederick R. Weisman Museum of Art Pepperdine University Malibu, California	January 8 - March 26, 2000
West Valley Art Museum/ Sun Cities Museum of Art Sun City, Arizona	August 18 - October 8, 2000

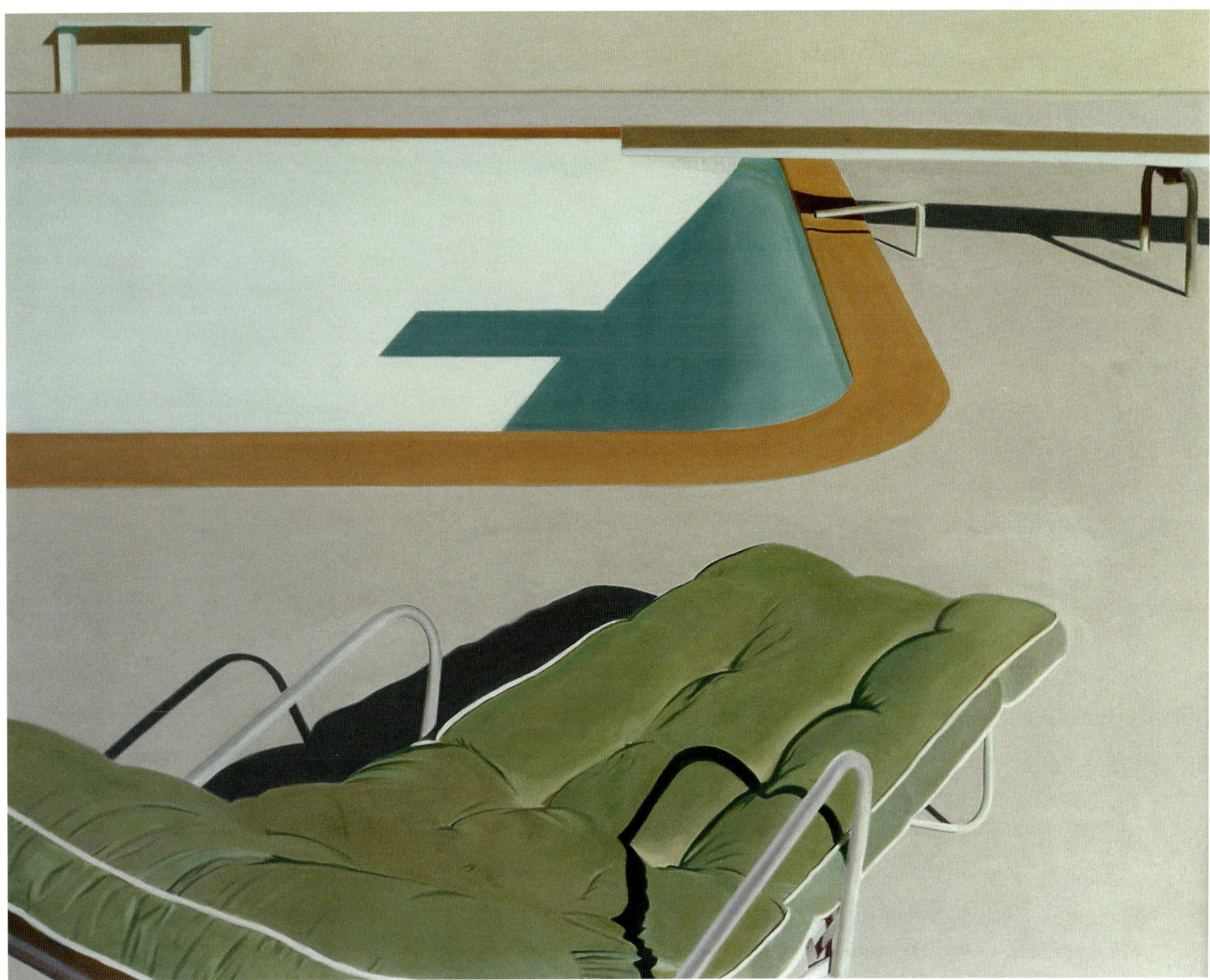

Foreword

Green Chair, 1976
oil on canvas, 40 x 40 inches
Collection of Tom Patchett,
Los Angeles

Opposite:
Venetian Light, 1977
oil on canvas, 42 x 49 1/4 inches
Collection of Mr. and Mrs.
Anthony Weir

The quiet, powerful presence of John Register's paintings caught my attention a number of years ago when I saw them at a gallery in San Francisco. I decided then to pursue the idea of having the San Jose Museum of Art mount a retrospective of the artist's body of work. Our guest curator, author Barnaby Conrad III, working with SJMA associate curator Cathy Kimball, has organized a comprehensive yet selective exhibition that offers insight into this painter's point of view and pinpoints his extraordinary ability to capture the pristine quality of light.

Sadly, John Register passed away in 1996. The sense of solitary reverie in his work now carries a poignancy that is underscored by his absence. This exhibition catalog, which includes a preface by Dr. Peter Selz, professor emeritus of art history at University of California at Berkeley, and an incisive essay by the artist's personal friend, Barnaby Conrad III, honors the beauty and strength of Register's work.

On behalf of the Museum's Trustees and the staff, I want to extend my gratitude to the many supporters and lenders to the exhibition who have so graciously agreed to part with their paintings for the San Jose presentation as well as the two-year national tour. We are particularly appreciative of Martin Muller and Katya Kashkooli of Modernism Gallery in San Francisco for their participation in organizing the exhibition and publishing the catalog. And, finally, we are deeply grateful to Cathy Register for her steadfast support — her spirit and enthusiasm have been invaluable throughout the realization of this project.

JOSI CALLAN
Director
San Jose Museum of Art

Preface

BY DR. PETER SELZ

Before his death in 1996 at the age of 57, John Register produced a distinctive body of work that established him as one of the important American realists of his generation. For a time Register was erroneously classified as a photo-realist largely because of the veristic style of his work. At first he was influenced by Richard Estes and Ralph Goings, who came to prominence in the late 1970s. But unlike these painters, Register did not treat the photographic image or slide as artifact; he used photographs merely as a starting point. Furthermore, the finish of his paintings is often quite loose and differs significantly from the smooth denials of visible brushwork that are characteristic of sharp-focus realists. Register built up his surfaces with multiple repainting and dramatic color adjustments, often painting out unnecessary details to strip a painting down to the essential visual statement.

Most important, his paintings do not look for an objective or neutral view of the visual world. He wrote: "A realist today must deal with the threat of the bomb, extraordinary materialist and Philistine values, a hypocritical government, and a generally vulgar environment. Consequently, the subject matter of a realist painter must capture the feeling of isolation, the tension of nothing happening. The suspended animation. The frozenness one feels when confronted with this environment."[1]

At first some of Register's work will remind the spectator of Edward Hopper's paintings of New York and New England. The artists share similar themes and a great interest in evoking an atmosphere of light. But Register, painting mostly in Los Angeles and the Southwest, captured a very different kind of light. He recorded the distinctive, diffuse atmosphere of this smoggy region between mountains and sea. In both artists' painting there is a sense of solitude, anomie and silence. Where Hopper's work dealt with the alienating effect of social relation-

Study for 'Desert Diner,' 1989
ink and charcoal, 14 x 11 inches
Private Collection

Opposite:
Interchange, 1993
oil on canvas, 50 x 50 inches
Collection of John and Barbara
Martin/Black Sparrow Press

ships, most of Register's paintings are void of human contact. Aware of the difference between his attitude and that of the older painter, Register affirmed that "with Hopper you witness someone else's isolation; in my pictures the viewer becomes the isolated one."[2] Register delineated the vacuity of Los Angeles in an unprecedented way. His pictures record the architecture of the time, but also a landscape of boredom, one in which lost and lonely misfits might be driven to violence, like the characters in Nathanael West's *The Day of The Locust*.

Speaking of Los Angeles, the eminent architectural historian Rayner Banham summed up this peculiar place when he observed, "the city will never be fully understood by those who cannot go with the flow of the unprecedented life." Register painted Los Angeles' impersonal freeways, lonely cafes and anonymous motels shadowed by scrubby palms, and his pictures evoke a passage of time similar to that captured by cinematic film stills.

Although remarkably consistent in vision, Register's style underwent subtle changes to accommodate the subjects he depicted. In stark early paintings such as *Overpass*, 1973, and *Manhattan Walking Bridge*, 1977, he not only refers back to American precisionists such as Charles Sheeler and Ralston Crawford, his sharply defined color planes make us think of hard-edge painters such as Ellsworth Kelly and John McLaughlin. By contrast, a decade later, he produced landscapes built up with many layers of pigment and visible brushstrokes, which relate to the Romantic tradition in American art.

Register's depictions of the Southland are not about fun in the sun. The recurring theme in his paintings is that of stark emptiness: empty chairs, empty rooms, empty cafes and empty lunch counters; train compartments and bus depots without passengers; and empty city streets that lead to empty highways and gas stations with no one pumping gas. There are many pictures of telephone booths with no one using the instrument. And yet occasionally a figure appears: a lonely man walking down a long road, a swimmer advancing with deliberate strokes toward a mysterious light, or, as in *Man on Bed*, 1995, one of the last paintings, a man sits upright and alone in a nameless hotel room. By keeping human beings out of his paintings, Register produced images that come close to those in Charles Sheeler's paintings. Both artists favored geometric clarity and established abstract patterns.

Manhattan Walking Bridge, 1977
oil on canvas, 50 x 35 inches
Collection of Ray Sinatra

Cadillac Hotel, 1984
oil on canvas, 50 x 70 inches
Collection of Mandy and
Cliff Einstein

In many of Register's paintings there are sets of objects, such as plastic chairs or dining tables, arranged in repetitive configurations. The philosopher Søren Kierkegaard spoke of patterns of recurrence as denoting fate ticking away, thus making us acutely aware of the limits of life. In 1984, soon after a desperate episode of illness, Register painted (and later silk-screened) a picture of a sunlit room titled *Waiting Room for the Beyond*. Here the intersecting precisionist patterns of light and shadow on the floor have an emotional charge as powerful as the lengthening shadows in De Chirico's metaphysical paintings. Slightly off-center sits an empty chair. As they are in so many of Register's pictures, this chair seems to be either waiting for an occupant or has just been vacated by someone. Beyond the bisected window we see clouds in the sky. It seems that this empty room with its spatial geometry has been projected into the realm of thought. Clearly, this artist's work went far beyond the self-imposed limitations of realism to reach for the spiritual.

Dr. Peter Selz is a professor emeritus of art history at the University of California at Berkeley.

JOHN REGISTER: PERSISTENT OBSERVER

BY BARNABY CONRAD III

John Register, 1994.
Photograph by Peter Register.

Introduction

The paintings of John Register (1939-1996) chronicle a search for overlooked beauty in unpeopled places. As a record of America's depersonalized landscapes, his paintings of empty coffee shops in Los Angeles, old hotels in Chicago and bus stations in the Southwestern desert celebrate sunlight, but also a haunting stillness tinged with regret and hope.

Though he called himself a realist, Register filtered the observed world through a tightly focused emotional lens. Often starting with snapshots of his subject, the artist absorbed and dramatically distilled early sketches until the finished painting appeared weeks or even years later bearing little resemblance to the original scene. His approach to painting is echoed in 20th century philosopher E.H. Gombrich's statement that, "There is no neutral naturalism...All art originated in the human mind, in our reactions to the world rather than in the visible world itself."[1]

In his last decade, many of Register's images came from the streets of Los Angeles, a city that, to him, epitomized the alienation of American life. "When I drive around L.A.," he said in 1989, "I look for an offbeat beauty. I don't know what I'm looking for until I find it. There are things so ugly that I can't paint them. Sometimes I get depressed by that city, and by other cities I visit. But I like the patina of things that have been battered by life."[2]

A persistent observer, Register claimed these places not just as American scenes but as expressions of a philosophical inner landscape. How much of that internal terrain he chose to reveal differed from painting to painting. If some pictures appear to be lonely or beautiful while others seem banal or startling, it is not by accident. Register was both attracted to and repelled by the architectural structures he found around him, and the pictures varied according to his health and emotional state.

Register came to art late in life, and his journey was an unusual one. Along the way he became a race car driver, top advertising art director, photographer, ten-

Wall Phone, 1991
oil on canvas, 50 x 35 inches
Collection of Les and Ginger Crane

Opposite:
Philippe's Sandwich Shop, 1984
oil on canvas, 50 x 70 inches
Courtesy of Molly Barnes and Joe Mock, Beverly Hills, California

Rest Area, 1989
oil on canvas, 40 x 50 inches
Private Collection

Opposite:
Pacific Rim Restaurant, 1989
oil on canvas, 50 x 70 inches
Collection of Winston
Stuart Conrad

nis fanatic, competitive chess player, compulsive letter writer and reader, ice-boat racer, backpacker, fisherman, surfer, and family man. During the last 16 years of his life he battled life-threatening illness and underwent grueling medical therapies. His struggle to stay alive gave him a sense of urgency, and drove him to make paintings that are rich with meaning and remarkably focused.

Though the West Coast informed Register's work, it would be an error to view him simply as a regionalist. As the late novelist and travel essayist Shiva Naipaul wrote in 1980, "California became, as it had to, the New World's New World, its last repository of hope. In California you come face to face with the Pacific and yourself. There is nowhere else to go."[3] Register's painted vision of California reminds us that the state anchors the western edge of the continent, a final, grand showcase for the American Dream. The artist was well aware of this, and wrote in 1989, "I feel the pressure of Des Moines, Cleveland, Detroit, Baltimore pushing behind me as I look out to sea. The teeming welter of humanity pushing."[4] While many of his images came from Los Angeles, his search for material took him all over the country, from the Great Plains to New York City.

Why did he choose to paint dingy restaurants and lowly cafes? "They are something we experience universally, a kind of common denominator of interior space," Register once said. "If I were to do my own house it would be too specific and not something that everybody can experience. But a cafe, hotel room or bus station — these are places we have all been before, places we can all relate to."[5]

The artist deliberately rejected obvious beauty to seek out another beyond the subject matter. "It's not beautiful furniture, it's all very ordinary," he once said. "It's as ordinary a chair as I could find. It's as ordinary a table as I could find. It's not that the ordinary chair is beautiful, but that in its ordinariness it becomes the essence of a chair, or the essence of a table."[6]

Register's art ventured beyond mere representation to conjure a metaphysical resonance from the commonplace. Viewed as examples of realism, these paintings are windows on the late 20th century. Received as the work of a philosophical artist, John Register's paintings ask us to contemplate the recent past, the fleeting present and the unknown future.

Early Life

John Sherman Register was born on February 1, 1939, in New York City, the last of three children of Samuel Croft Register and Dorothy Pratt Register. His parents were from old New England families, Episcopalian in culture and upbringing. They divorced when he was 3.

Register moved to the Los Angeles area in 1942 following his mother's marriage to William Barrett, an Army psychiatrist stationed in Santa Monica. They lived in a rented house on the Pacific Coast Highway near Ocean Park. World War II was at its peak and California was a center for troop shipments to the Pacific Campaign against the Japanese. As a child Register was aware of the war effort, of the rumors of Japanese submarines off the coast, and of the strangely beautiful California landscape in which he had landed.

"We had anti-aircraft guns and sandbag bunkers on the beach in front of our house," Register wrote of his childhood. "My memories of Southern California span 50 years. I remember driving on Sunset [Boulevard] and my recollection is there were no houses, just ochre hills of dried grass. When I see Southern California now I can't help but be tinged with a sense of loss; a lost childhood, and a lost way of life. Perhaps some of this is in my painting."[1]

Along with his brother Sam and sister Barbara, Register spent summers visiting his father, a yacht broker in Marion, Massachusetts. "I was always interested in drawing. My father did some illustrations for *Yachting* magazine on a casual basis, and once he drew India ink silhouettes of square-riggers on a lamp that intrigued me as a child. Drawing was the one thing I could do better than the other kids."[2]

The margins of Register's notebooks from school were riddled with images of World War II dogfights and other doodles, but for the most part his early drawings were not connected with any notion of art.

Pacific Coast Highway, 1990
oil on paper, 11 x 15 inches
Collection of Martin Muller

Opposite: John Register, 1963.
Photograph by Mario Tosi.

Register's relationship with Samuel Register Sr. was complicated by their geographical separation and by his father's alcoholism and liver and pancreatic cancer. At age 11, Register spent a "troublesome" summer with his father that ended with them quarreling in a rainstorm before John was put on the airplane home. As an adult he recalled their parting in a letter: "On the plane, trying to look out the window, I knew I would never see him again. I was crying. The airplane engine throttled up. Rain drops swept horizontally past on the window glass and past that it was black. He was gone.... that summer they had discovered cancer in his lymph nodes. I had always assumed that I had caused my father such displeasure he didn't want me back in the summers. Now I think he was trying to say good-bye, that he would never see me again."[3] His father died a few months later.

After the war, Register's mother and stepfather moved to the San Francisco Bay Area, where they added a third son, Stephen Barrett, to the family. "The biggest influence in my youth was my mother," said Register. "A strong, independent woman, she was used to running things her own way. She imparted to me a clear sense of right and wrong and a healthy dose of the work ethic."[4] Dorothy Barrett ran a large horse farm in Morgan Hill until she was well into her 80s, and outlived two of her sons, dying in 1998 at the age of 89. She was proud of her ancestors, particularly Roger Sherman, who helped draft and sign the Declaration of Independence and later served as a U.S. Senator from Connecticut (1791-93). Her eldest son, Sam, shared her love of horses and went on to become a nationally ranked equestrian and horse-show judge.

Register described his childhood as one of "benign neglect," and never felt at home in this formal world. As a young adult he rejected it by becoming a working professional. "It's not a background that encourages writing and art," he wrote. "I had to try and turn my back on it, and when I did the world became a strange place, and I needed to document it."[5] A friend and fellow artist, Thomas Quinn, remembered that Dorothy Barrett's life of horse shows and country clubs was "a world John rejected wholeheartedly; he always sought the underdog position. He never liked unearned favor."

From San Mateo, California, John was sent to the East Coast at 13 to attend Brooks School. He was miserable. "It was strict, modeled after the old English

Abandoned Chair, circa 1960.
Photograph by John Register.

View of L.A., 1980
oil on canvas, 25 x 35 inches
Collection of Mrs. Helen Schacter

public school. We had to take mass cold showers and the prefects, older boys, dished out discipline as they pleased. It was really like *Lord of the Flies.*"[6]

At 15 he transferred to The Lawrenceville School in New Jersey, where he spent three years and was graduated in 1957. There he was an average student and played exuberant fourth-string football, but he also became art editor of the school's literary magazine. One of his cartoons depicted a goofy prep school kid lighting his way "down the tunnel of existence" with a lantern in whose rays were written "Religion IV." (In 1980, he revisited the school and was delighted to see the cartoon still being used as a spot illustration in the literary magazine.) He also drew semi-erotic drawings of women, one of which, an image of "an almond-eyed sex-kitten," he showed to the headmaster's wife, rakishly asking her if the feminine anatomy was correct. He joined Lawrenceville's Easel Club, which offered trips to Manhattan to visit the Metropolitan Museum and the Museum of Modern Art.

He befriended Deny McCoy, a schoolmate whose uncle was Andrew Wyeth. One day, McCoy and his sister Ann (who later became a portrait painter) invited Register to visit Wyeth at his studio in Chadd's Ford, Pennsylvania. "We sat in a circle drawing one another. Tacked to the wall of the studio was a list of people waiting to buy a painting from Wyeth. I remember he was working on that famous painting of the dead deer hanging from a tree in winter. I saw all the beautiful preliminary sketches. Wyeth explained it was a radical composition for him and asked what I thought. 'It looks good to me,' I said. And I thought, 'What an incredible life it must be to be a painter.'"[7]

Register's closest boyhood friend in California during the 1950s was Hunt Barclay, who was already showing significant talent as a painter. Barclay had an ease with landscapes that John admired. "We did some painting together," he recalled. "Hunt was incredibly gifted. In a way I think my contact with Andrew Wyeth and my friendship with Hunt Barclay inhibited me, as I felt I just wasn't born with enough natural ability."[8]

Barclay went on to study with Frank Mason, a New York artist who emulated the old masters. (Ironically, Barclay gave up his own painting career to manufacture sporting apparel just about the time Register gave up business to become an

Register first thought of becoming an artist while visiting Andrew Wyeth's studio circa 1956, where he saw watercolors similar to Wyeth's *Hanging Deer*, 1961. (Study for *Tenant Farmer*, 1961)
21 3/4 x 13 7/8 inches
Collection of Mrs. Andrew Wyeth

Club Delta, 1973
oil on canvas, 16 x 24 inches
Private Collection

artist.) "I had a facility with paint," Barclay observed years later, "but I didn't have the poetic vision that John had."

Barclay's early memories of Register are of a teen-ager who saw life as a great adventure, a game that wasn't fun unless it was filled with risk and humor. Back home in California, Register would often accompany Barclay and his mother Wendy Howell on their aging houseboat, *Squarehead*, for voyages up to the Sacramento River Delta. Anchored near the town of Terminus, the boys spent their days jumping off the local bridge into the tepid muddy water 35 feet below, water-skiing naked back and forth in front of the girls who worked in a tomato-picking plant, and then swaggering into the Terminus Bar for an illegal beer. "We were 15, but we got served," remembered Barclay. "We would sit and stare fondly at a painting over the bar of a lady with six breasts, three in each vertical row down her chest. The picture was so realistic that to this day we talk about it as a symbol of abundant womanhood." [An early Register painting, *Club Delta*, 1973 (above), depicts the neon sign of yet another riverside tavern.]

When the boys were 16, Barclay's mother allowed them to take the houseboat on their own. Once while Barclay was water-skiing behind their runabout, Register swerved the boat sharply and yelled a warning. "A moment later I saw why," recalled Barclay. "I flashed by an alligator at least 7 feet long. That big reptile bashed the water with his tail and headed for the bottom of the slough. When we went back to the Terminus Bar and told the story, no one believed us, because alligators don't live in the Delta. The next day we were vindicated when it came out in the papers that a large alligator had been stolen from the Sacramento Zoo."

Barclay recalled a night after a beer party when he and John fell into a heavy slumber in their sleeping bags, which they had unrolled atop air mattresses. "We were right next to the river's edge. For some reason, maybe the full moon, the river rose about 3 feet that night. Awakened by the sunlight, I rolled off my mattress, and fell into the river! I looked back and saw we had floated a quarter mile downstream from the houseboat. John was still asleep, snoring heavily in mid-river, floating slowly to San Francisco. I hated to wake him up."[9]

In 1957 Register enrolled at the University of California at Berkeley, where he majored in English. "I didn't take any art courses because the teachers taught Abstract Expressionism," he explained. "Majoring in art seemed flaky."[10] Nevertheless, he continued making drawings and watercolors on his own.

The Berkeley campus in the 1950s was not known as a breeding ground for artists. James Shinn, who later served as deputy ambassador to Switzerland, remembered meeting Register as a "pledge" to the Zeta Psi fraternity house in 1958. Now 6 feet 3 inches tall, Register was charismatic, and popular with young women. Though it was clear to Shinn that the dark-haired youth was a natural leader, he "marched to the beat of a different drummer," and within a year Register moved out of the fraternity house. Shinn wrote, "I thought his major in English and fey sense of humor might lead to writing — not painting." The paintings that Register eventually produced, Shinn commented, showed he had "an uncanny ability in observing America and its culture. ...critical but non-judgmental....people seem to recognize that he is saying that behind the surface glitter of the 'American Way of Life' lies a deep sadness, but he says this with deep compassion."[11]

Register's intense interest in literature extended to theater. Philadelphia playwright Tom Bissinger recalled that as Berkeley freshmen he and Register discovered "the world of existentialism" when they crossed the Bay Bridge in 1958 to

Register attended a 1957 performance of Beckett's *Waiting For Godot* in San Francisco. Collection of San Francisco Main Library

Register spent a semester studying art in Paris in 1960.

attend a production of Samuel Beckett's "Waiting For Godot" at the Actor's Workshop in San Francisco. "We felt we were witnessing the birth of something new, fresh, disturbing, raucous, mad," Bissinger said. "It was art, psychology and theater of the absurd rolled into one, and it was very, very real." Register and Bissinger also amused themselves by quoting the poetry of e.e. cummings.[12]

In his junior year at Berkeley, Register took a semester abroad to study painting at the Académie Julian in Paris. "I thought that was where you went to study art," he said. "I took some seascapes in a suitcase to the Ecole des Beaux-Arts, but they wouldn't accept me. So I went to the Académie Julian. We painted from the model, and I enjoyed shaking hands with everyone each morning in the French tradition: *Bon jour, ça va, bon jour, ça va.*"

Register lived in the old Hôtel d'Alsace, a seedy relic in the Rue des Beaux Arts, where Oscar Wilde had lived and died. He ate most of his meals at the nearby Café des Beaux-Arts in the Rue Bonaparte, where he had his own wooden napkin ring reserved. "I found an English bookstore down by the Seine, and as

Register frequented Left Bank cafes like the Balzar. Collection of Martin Muller

important as it was for me to paint every day, I think it was equally important that for the first time I was able to read books without being worried about being quizzed on their content." He read omnivorously. A week's typical fare included the autobiography of Bevenuto Cellini, works by Proust, and Somerset Maugham's *Of Human Bondage* and *The Razor's Edge*. "Upton Sinclair's *The Jungle* and *Oil!* were good socialist novels to heighten a youth's social consciousness in the stupor of the Eisenhower years," Register noted.

At night he hung out at the Nuage, a scabrous Rive Gauche bar frequented by artists and writers. "James Jones and William Styron came in a lot. It was probably the only bar where Henry Moore's work ever inspired a fist fight. It started when I was sitting at the bar next to Frank Norman, a tough Cockney who had just written a hit play in London called 'Fings Ain't Wot They Used T' Be.' He was drunk and belligerent. 'You're trying to be an artist,' he snarled at me. 'You know Henry Moore's work?' 'Sure,' I said. 'He does the folks with holes in them.' That was all it took."

It was a romantic winter and spring for a young American in Paris. "Edith Piaf songs played everywhere. The scent of Gauloises cigarettes floated in the air. I was an expatriate art student, and it was great until I was asked to leave the country for protesting France's involvement in Algeria. The French police were very polite about it. I promised I would not become embroiled in the waning years of French colonialism in Africa, and they let me stay."[13]

In 1961 Register began to race cars in autocrosses and hill climbs. Photograph by Catherine Register.

On his return to Berkeley, Register continued to sketch and spent two summers working for a silk-screening company in Burlingame that produced American flags. He also studied at the California School of Fine Arts in San Francisco with Elmer Bischoff and Nathan Oliveira, who were part of the Figurative Expressionist school emerging in the Bay Area. Bischoff gave Register an F in painting. "I was unresponsive, maybe rebellious toward their type of painting and teaching," Register conceded. Many years later, Register saw a painting by Bischoff at the San Francisco Museum of Modern Art. "I thought it was a masterpiece. I wish at 19 I could have comprehended what he was teaching."[14]

In his youth, Register's energies were as often focused on action as art. After graduation from Berkeley in 1961, he enrolled in the Sports Car Club of America's

Register raced cars all over California and set a number of course records. Photograph by Catherine Register.

California race-drivers' school. Aided by a college buddy named Chuck Eastman, he took up car racing seriously. Enlisting a Japanese mechanic, he souped up a 1954 Austin Healy and began to compete in autocrosses, quickly moving up to hill climbs. "We were fanatics," Register recalled. "I set the record for the Georgetown Hill Climb for Class E production cars. In the process we beat a lot of bigger cars: Ferrari, Jaguar, small Corvettes.... Then I moved to road racing."

Racing in California in the 1960s was much different from the sport today. "We raced on old asphalt airport landing strips. I can still smell the greaseweed, alfalfa, creosote, Castrol X, high-octane fuel perfume. The drivers' meetings were held on hay bales. The morning of the race, the evening dew would still be holding the dust down, an announcer would be listening to the sound of his voice over the engine blips of early morning tuners, making sure it would carry to the 20 fans that would assemble in the bleachers. Soon it would be intensely hot and the end of the straightaway would shimmer like a mirage." The racers would camp out in tents in the infield, occasionally with girlfriends.[15]

Register and his pit crew wore special tags, which gave them access to the race track and its infield.

Among his rivals on the circuit were Lance Reventlow and actor Steve McQueen. His friend and occasional mechanic, Thomas Quinn, remembered that unlike the well-known drivers, Register favored the role of the dark horse and used it to strategic advantage. "John and his car looked like they had come to the race course half-asleep and still in rumpled pajamas," Quinn said. "He had a nasty-sounding little Porsche Speedster, milky white with blotches of mildew-green and gray primer on its bruised haunches, with its race numbers peeling away — like one of his decaying-hotel paintings. Speed secrets had been breathed into the engine, and together they went very fast."

In one race, Quinn recalled, Register came from behind, overtaking 29 cars, and tailing an E-Type Jaguar, a Lotus Super 7 and a lovely silver Speedster. Hectored by Register, the Jag spun on the last turn, and John finished second in class and ninth overall. "As his Porsche came to a rest, a metallic stink rose from the car. That's how we learned that he'd run the last half of the race without front brakes."[16] (Quinn felt that this story was a metaphor for Register's life as a late-starting artist.) Although there was still no real thought in his mind of becoming a professional artist, in idle moments Register sketched endless doodles of "rear engine monsters" on notepads.

Off the track, he had started working in the management training program of McCann-Erickson in San Francisco. "That is, I worked in the mailroom and pushed a mail cart around to everyone's desk. Then I got into print production, where I learned type-specing and the rudiments of layout design." Fortunately, an art director named Charles Eckart (destined to become an artist himself), suggested Register study commercial art at the Art Center in Los Angeles. He enrolled immediately.

In a photography class at the Art Center, Register met Catherine Richards. "The assignment was to pair off and photograph another student. Cathy was the prettiest girl in the class, so I grabbed her." There were parallels in their lives: Both were born in New York at Children's Hospital, and both lost their fathers at age 11. Cathy's father, a Princeton-educated doctor who had served in New Guinea during World War II, had died at age 48 of heart disease. Brought up in Laguna

Register, 1963.
Photograph by Catherine Register.

Opposite:
Cathy, 1963.
Photograph by John Register.

Beach, California, she, like Register, was sent east to school. Both had a rebellious streak. And both had a great love of art and photography.

They were married five months later, on February 6, 1964, in Manhattan, and Register gave up car racing forever. He channeled his competitive spirit into advertising. That year the young couple moved to Brooklyn. Register studied design and television production at Pratt Institute, an art school founded in 1887 by his great-grandfather, Charles Pratt. (Register was the first member of his family to attend the school.) He soon joined the advertising firm Young & Rubicam. After a stint as a graphic designer at Elektra Films, he went back to advertising and within a few years developed into a seasoned and successful art director, producing television commercials all over the world.

Register, however, had mixed feelings about his career on Madison Avenue. "I hated working in advertising, yet I realize now that it taught me some important skills. Notably to distinguish between art and illustration. I like some illustration, but it is supposed to make a point, to send a message. I believe a successful painting does *not* make a point or send a message. A good painting has an ineffable, mysterious quality, it eschews technique, and it is a refinement of the commonplace."[17]

Brooklyn Chess Club, 1964.
Photograph by Catherine Register.

His passion for chess drew him to the Brooklyn Chess Club and the New York Commercial Chess League. His love of 19th-century chess gambits led to many entertaining games, and a few upsets with better players. He played in a number of tournaments, including the New York State championships. "Chess is the most democratic of games. All you can bring to it is your mind." He pursued the pastime all his life, and eventually taught his children to play.

In New York Register worked for a number of ad agencies. His career peaked with a promotion to senior vice-president of McCaffrey & McCall. While most of his energy was spent creating television commercials for clients such as Quaker Oats and Exxon, he continued to take a Saturday class at the Art Students League and painted small landscapes on Sundays. The first of the Registers' three children, Peter, was born on August 27, 1965, followed by Kate in 1966 and David in 1969.

McCaffrey & McCall prospered and went public. Register owned stock in the company, but in 1970 he cashed out his shares to become a professional photographer. He and his family packed their 1966 Volvo and drove across the coun-

Cafe, San Francisco at 3 a.m., 1971
Photographic series by John Register.

try to San Francisco, where he worked as a photographer for *Sunset* magazine and the *San Francisco Examiner*. He shot stories like "San Francisco at 3 a.m." (a photo essay on the city's graveyard-shift workers) and covered a film festival for pornographic movie stars. "I did a fashion assignment in Banff. I shot for *Earth* magazine. I even did work for advertising agencies," he recalled. "But after awhile I saw it was crazy. I just felt like I was a button-pusher illustrating someone else's bad ideas."[18]

The photographs he made of pre-dawn San Francisco were bleak, quirky and abstract, relating to work by photographers such as Lee Friedlander and Robert Frank. These shots of cafes and storefronts, however, remarkably prefigure Register's future paintings in content and composition.

A year later, the Registers moved back to New York and John became an associate creative director at the advertising firm of Ogilvy & Mather. "David Ogilvy operated the firm almost like the British Army, with separate luncheon rooms for the 'officers' and for the 'enlisted men.' I was one of the few art directors who was head of a creative group, a division within the firm that Ogilvy called a 'syndicate,' in the British manner. I had, among others, the Schweppes account. Ogilvy

Hotel Atlanta, San Francisco at 3 a.m., 1971

TV Chair, San Francisco at 3 a.m., 1971

himself had created the campaign. My first day I was in the 'officer's mess' and Ogilvy sat down next to me. He turned to me with his clipped British accent and asked: 'Why is it that we are paying you so much more than we did the chap who used to do your job?' I answered him, 'If you *had* paid him more he wouldn't have left.' In retrospect, whatever they could have paid me wouldn't have been enough. Ogilvy himself was no longer involved with the day-to-day operation of the agency. The authority was delegated to some hard-eyed bureaucrats. The agency had become a boring place to work, with all the manufactured hysteria of getting a campaign done or pitching a new account."[19]

A friend and colleague, Eugene Beck, rendered this portrait of the artist as a young advertising man: "On his better days he could take on a group of the best their sort could muster in much the manner Bruce Lee defended a 360-degree battle perimeter... He knew their language far better than they and possessed a mind so much keener that while they squirmed, skewered on their own misfiring synapses, he was on to the next meeting, an absorbing chess game, or we were already walking our nightly route uptown along Fifth or Madison."[20]

On the surface, it seemed like a fine life. Register had a beautiful wife and three children, a Fifth Avenue apartment and high career prospects. Yet he was unhappy, wretched. "I was almost speechless with misery about my job and life. Sometimes Cathy and I would go to the Museum of Modern Art to look at the paintings during lunch. One time I remember telling her that if only I could paint one good picture, I might be happy."

Shortly after his 33rd birthday, in 1972, an event occurred that changed his life. "We were in the conference room for yet another big meeting concerning the Sears account," Register recalled. "They were preparing me, like [the character in] *The Manchurian Candidate*, to go to Chicago again to discuss some inane project. I saw that this was the way my whole life would be in advertising. I realized that I just couldn't do it. I stood up and said, 'I'm sorry, I have a dentist appointment. I have to leave.' They all looked at me quizzically. I left the meeting, left a note for my boss, and never went back to an office."

It was mid-afternoon when he got home. The apartment was empty. His wife was in the park with the kids. Register went out to find her. She was surprised to

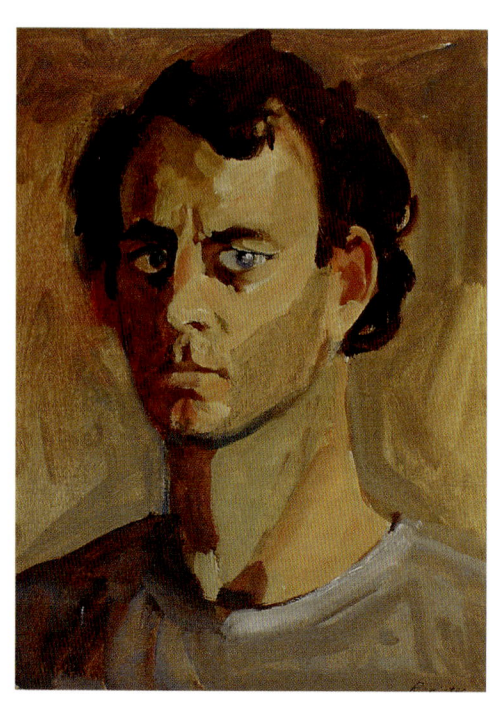

Self-portrait, 1971
oil on cardboard, 16 x 12 inches
Collection of Catherine Register

see him. "I just quit," he said. She wasn't shocked. "Now what am I going to do?" he pondered aloud. "You always wanted to run around the reservoir," she answered. "Why not try it?"

"It was true," remembered Register. "Every morning as I dressed for work I'd look out the window and see the joggers. They ran in rain and snow. They were a symbol of the intrepid for me. So I ran around the reservoir that afternoon."[21]

Girl on the Chaise, 1973
oil on canvas, 40 x 60 inches
Collection of Catherine Register

Running became a ritual for Register, whose body weight dropped from 195 to a lean 165 pounds. Cathy bought him an easel. He pulled out his paints and brushes, and within a week he was running and painting every day. He studied for three months at the Art Students League with Everett Raymond Kinstler, the portrait painter. After a few months at the League, he completed a panoramic painting of the model on her podium and all the students toiling at their easels. "Ray Kinstler, whose praise was rare, one day pointed at my painting and said, 'I like the way you've painted that foot.'"

He also studied with Lennart Anderson, the landscape painter. "I was using a strange palette, mostly browns. Anderson came up to me, pointed to a brownish shadow area on the nude I was painting, and said, 'What is this? It looks like beetle juice.' He took my brush and palette and mixed up chrome oxide green and vermilion and began painting right on my canvas. I was offended at first, but I learned to see color in a different way. There is exciting color in even the darkest shadow."

Sometimes riding the bus downtown to the Art Students League, Register would run into ad executives he had worked with. "They would be dressed in their three-piece suits and sleek leather attaché cases while I'd be in blue jeans carrying my grubby paintbox. Even if we said hello, I had the feeling they thought I was disreputable, weird, maybe even degenerate."[22] Though his future was uncertain, Register felt that for the first time in his life he was doing what really counted.

First Paintings

John Register painted his first major painting, *Cadillac Grill with Flags*, 1973 (opposite), with great difficulty. "It took me over two months to finish it because I planned it badly and had to repaint it five times to get the surface right. I was making the jump from art-school life classes to what I hoped would be a finished painting. I was teaching myself to paint the hard way."

He explained the car imagery. "Just coming out of drawing classes at the Art Students League, I was pretty open to influence from other artists. [The magazine] *Art In America* did a big issue on photo-realists like Richard Estes and Ralph Goings. The car was a celebrated icon in America. So I took my shot at it, too."[1] *Cadillac Grill*'s double image of the American flag may also reflect an interest in the flag paintings of Jasper Johns. Later that year Register completed *Faded Flag* (right), showing a windblown Stars and Stripes, but few of his later paintings would focus tightly on objects as icons.

He finished a half-dozen paintings in 1973, notably a large canvas called *Overpass* (p. 44). The bold diagonal composition and industrial theme of the picture relates to the works of Charles Sheeler and Ralston Crawford, but the scale is more in line with the large abstractions and Pop Art (such as Robert Cottingham's work) that Register saw in galleries and museums during those years.

Although he sold a few paintings to friends, Register soon realized that without a salary he couldn't afford the apartment on Fifth Avenue. At the same time, Cathy's mother, who lived in California, became ill. So in 1973, the Registers once again packed up the Volvo and drove across the country, first to Laguna Beach, then to settle in Malibu at Point Dume. They took a tree-shrouded house on a street called Bison Court (just a block from the house that the Register family currently owns).

Register surfed with his sons Peter and David, riding waves at Malibu, Hanalei Bay in the Hawaiian Islands, and Todos Santos near Cabo San Lucas, Mexico. He

Opposite:
Cadillac Grill with Flags, 1973
oil on canvas, 32 x 50 inches
Private Collection

Faded Flag, 1973
oil on canvas, 16 x 20 inches
Collection of George and Beth Gage

Register with *Overpass*,
New York, 1973. Photograph
by Catherine Register.

Overpass, 1973
oil on canvas, 35 x 50 inches
Courtesy of Modernism Gallery,
San Francisco

played tennis intensely and coached his children on a local Malibu soccer team, the Rattlers. He was a caring father and husband, and an affable host with his friends, a number of them artists.

In these early California years Register completed important works drawing on subject matter that he would return to throughout his life. *Four Telephone Booths*, 1975 (opposite), was his first picture utilizing a serial approach to objects. The booths are ostensibly identical, but each is slightly differentiated, either by the shape of a shadow or placement of a phone book. Register acknowledged that he was interested in the serial imagery of Andy Warhol and Wayne Thiebaud, but also pointed out that this kind of repetition occurs constantly in American life. The motivation for the telephone picture, however, was deeply personal.

"I used to have a recurring nightmare, that I was in a mental institution and that I was sane," he said. "The more I tried to demonstrate my sanity, the more hysterical my voice and my behavior became. The closer I came to acting like an

Four Phone Booths, 1974
oil on canvas, 40 x 60 inches
Private Collection

insane person the less the doctors believed me. In the dream there is always a phone booth, which represents a link to sanity. The only way to get back to the real world. So when I saw these four phone booths one day while I was walking along a street in L.A., they appealed to me not only for their serial aspect, but because of that dream."²

Hotel With Four Chairs, 1974 (opposite), was one of Register's first major interior-exterior paintings. In this work, four armchairs face a large window with a view of a city street. (An oil-on-paper sketch of the work included a man in a hat, but this figure was eliminated in the final version.) The empty chairs, like ghostly senti-

Mustang Cafe, 1975
oil on canvas, 33 x 43 inches
Collection of George and
Beth Gage

Opposite:
Hotel with Four Chairs, 1974
oil on canvas, 45 x 45 inches
Collection of Martin Muller

Quality Cafe, 1977
oil on canvas, 33 x 54 1/2 inches
Collection of Mr. and Mrs. Anthony Weir

Opposite:
Closed Restaurant, 1975
oil on canvas, 50 x 50 inches
Collection of Harvey Mudd

nels, remind us of the forlorn lives that come and go in seedy downtown hotels. The window separates the interior from the bleak world outside. During the next 20 years, empty chairs would appear dozens of times in his work.

The artist painted a series of cafe pictures, beginning with *Mustang Cafe* (p. 47), followed by *Closed Restaurant* (opposite) and *Quality Cafe* (above). "*Quality Cafe* actually exists in the Wilshire area of Los Angeles," said Register. "I'd been looking for subject matter early in the morning and I wandered into this local place for my coffee and doughnut. I thought, 'This is a wonderful cafe.' I always keep a small camera in my pocket. As I photographed it, a painting started in my head."[3]

Register's cafe pictures fall within a genre of interior-exterior pictures that stretches back to Pieter de Hooch and Jan Vermeer and up to Edward Hopper,

Richard Diebenkorn and Richard Estes, all of whom Register admired. "The art history aside, I realized that the interior-exterior thing was important to me. In *Mustang Cafe*, you see intimate things like coffee cups on the table, while outside are less personal things like parking meters and cars. There is something threatening about the American street. The interior is a haven, a symbol of safety, a resting place, while outside there is an alien world. So I use cold, acid colors outside, and warm colors inside."[4]

From 1973 through 1975, Register painted every day, without feedback, in his solitary studio. "It was a time of great self-doubt for him," recalled Cathy. By 1975 he had produced 10 paintings that he thought were good enough to show to a gallery. He had no idea how to convince a dealer to display his work, so he drove up and down La Cienaga Boulevard with all the pictures in the back of the Volvo. "I ended up at the David Stuart Gallery," said Register. "They gave me a show and we sold six paintings. That was the beginning."[5]

Inspired by Randy's Donuts, Santa Monica, Register removed the large donut sign in the final painting (opposite page). Photograph by Peter Register, 1998.

Drive-through Donut Shop, 1975
oil on canvas, 31 x 49 inches
Collection of Catherine Register

One of Register's signature motifs was chairs. He completed his second single-chair painting, *Yellow Chair* (opposite), in 1977. "I had just finished reading a book by Johannes Itten, a Bauhaus color master who greatly influenced Josef Albers," he said. "What he said made sense to me, putting colors together like musical notes to make a chord. I tried to make paintings based on a key color and would work around it, trying to build harmony."[6]

When Stuart gave him a second show, in 1977, *Los Angeles Times* critic Henry J. Seldis wrote that Register was "an extraordinary painter whose external realism is based on metaphysical and psychological concepts along with a highly persuasive manner of painting." Seldis called Register's handling of light and shadow "masterful."[7] It was a nice start for an unknown 38-year-old artist.

Register pursued the serial theme in *Oxnard Pizza*, 1978 (p. 54), and *Red Booths* (p. 55) of the same year. In *Red Booths* the perspective and candy-apple red color are almost overwhelming. "I didn't just paint booths in that picture. The metaphor is probably obvious," he said. "I remember myself as a teen-ager sliding into those booths — everyone slid into them. There's a sex thing about it. The thighs of young girls sticking to the smooth red plastic booths, generations of thighs have stuck to them. The booths recede back to a seemingly endless vanishing point, symbolizing the repetition of a common human experience: the full lust of adolescence. Experiences that we think are highly individual are in fact experienced over and over."[8]

Some of the hotels and cafes that Register painted evoke images from books by Los Angeles novelists Raymond Chandler, Nathanael West and John Fante. The artist, however, disclaimed an interest in nostalgia. "It just happens that these old-time places in Venice are what I'm used to, and they are being torn down. I went back to one hotel in Venice I painted a few years ago and it had been replaced by a center that does performance art — whatever that is. There's a fragility to the urban fabric in L.A. that people aren't aware of. I'm attracted to places where real life has taken place."[9]

Hollywood Hornet, 1975
oil on canvas, 32 x 50 inches
Collection of Robert Solomon

Opposite:
Yellow Chair, 1977
oil on canvas, 50 x 50 inches
Collection of Diane and
Tom Yohe

Red Booths, 1978
oil on canvas, 46 1/2 x 72 inches
Collection of Mr. and Mrs.
Peter Asher

Opposite:
Oxnard Pizza, 1978
oil on canvas, 45 x 45 inches
Collection of Margret Jhin Walsh
and Peter A. Walsh

Big Brother, 1976
oil on canvas, 35 x 50 inches
Collection of The Most Reverend
Robert S. and Mrs. Morse

Motel, 1977
oil on canvas, 50 x 50 inches
Collection of Catherine Register

Very few of Register's pictures could be construed as political except *Big Brother*, 1976 (left). The picture's title refers, of course, to the omniscient, ubiquitous ruler in George Orwell's novel *1984*, but the looming billboard bearing a politician's face is less a totalitarian threat than just another hollow media gesture. In an earlier version of *Big Brother*, John clearly painted in the name of the billboarded politician, William Matson Roth, heir to a Pacific shipping fortune, a Democrat who was running for governor.[10] Register knew Roth slightly, identified with his politics, but painted out the name to make a generalized statement about politicians who come and go.

Although he was a realist who used photos as a point of departure, Register was not a photo-realist painter. "Rendering from a photograph in a photo-realist manner would be so boring, I couldn't do it. It would be torture. For me, painting is less rendering and more distillation. I try to reduce an image to its essence."[11]

For example, in *Closed Restaurant*, 1975, Register painted a cafe so empty, so devoid of activity, that he painted no salt and pepper in the shakers, and no napkins in the tabletop dispensers. He even felt that the poorer the photograph he worked from, the better the painting turned out. Occasionally he photocopied photographs to reduce them to simplified shapes of light and dark.

Speaking about another early painting, *Mojave Pool*, 1976 (p. 11), the artist recalled, "The pool was at a hotel in the Mojave Desert, and it was an uncharacteristically hot day in the winter. Apparently the people that ran the motel didn't have enough clients to keep the pool filled out of season…. Although the photograph had to be taken through a chain-link fence which obscured a lot of the information, my painting probably turned out better than if I had made a technically good photograph, because I was forced to generalize."[12]

Register saw the swimming pool as an archetype of Los Angeles. "Years after I painted *Mojave Pool*," he said, "I came across this quote in Chandler's *The Long Goodbye*: 'Off to my left there was an empty swimming pool and nothing ever looks emptier than an empty swimming pool.'"[13] But where an artist like David Hockney painted swimming pools at private houses — as symbols of status — Register focused on motel pools, facilities that the general public would frequent.

Olive Motel, 1978
oil on canvas, 27 x 39 inches
Private Collection

The pool painting's strength comes from a bold sense of light and shadow rather than slavishly rendered details. It is the composition, not the rendering, that makes the picture work. Register once said, "I tend to agree with Fairfield Porter, who said that every realist painting has to be judged on its abstract merits."[14]

The inspiration for *Parking Lot by the Ocean*, 1976 (opposite), was just as spontaneous as the conception of the pool and café paintings. "I was driving along the Pacific Coast Highway, looked over and saw this parked Cadillac and a man lying in his lounge chair near the sea. It meant something to me, so I stopped and took a photograph. It's one of the ironies of Southern California that the climate is beautiful with sub-tropical foliage, and yet there is always this reminder that we are ruining our environment with our headlong greed. So I painted a band of copper-colored sulfurous smog just on the horizon line. It's paradise gone amok."[15] All of Register's paintings in 1977 were of Los Angeles or the West except *Manhattan Walking Bridge* (p. 16), a reminder of his New York days.

Study #2 for 'Parking Lot by the Ocean,' 1976
Pencil on paper, 12 x 17 inches
Collection of Barnaby Conrad III

Parking Lot by the Ocean, 1976
oil on canvas, 31 x 48 inches
Collection of Peter E. Thieriot

Top: The Register family, 1978.

Above: Surfing at Cabo San Lucas, 1978.

Opposite:
Laundromat, 1983
oil on canvas, 50 x 50 inches
Collection of Morgan Flagg and Elizabeth Ross Flagg

Previous pages: *Santa Ana Motor Parts*, 1979
oil on canvas, 25 1/2 x 60 inches
Collection of Charles and Kay Lowe

Register was once (somewhat inaccurately) called "a kind of West Coast Edward Hopper."[16] A clear difference in their approach to painting was noted by *San Francisco Chronicle* art critic Kenneth Baker: "Register weighs the aspects of his pictures very differently from the way Hopper did. For Hopper, subtleties of light and color were always secondary to the metaphoric and emotional content of a picture. For Register, they are primary."[17]

Register didn't much mind the comparison. "I love Hopper's work. We see things similarly, but we're different. He sets up disenfranchised people on a kind of pictorial stage that projects a sense of isolation. With Hopper you witness someone else's isolation; in my pictures, I think you, the viewer, become the isolated one."[18] Register added: "There is a psychological connection, but there is absolutely no connection in the way we put the paint down."[19]

Register was included in a group exhibition called "Cityscapes" at the Fine Arts Museums of San Francisco in 1977. The following year he had a one-man show at the William Sawyer Gallery in San Francisco, and in 1979 the Boehm Gallery in San Diego gave him a solo exhibition.

Although the West Coast, and especially Los Angeles, was coming of age as a cultural scene, Register once again looked back to New York. Having worked on his own for more than five years, he now wanted to see what it would be like to live in an artists' community. So in the summer of 1979 the Registers drove across the country to Long Island and rented a drafty old house in East Hampton. This community had been a haven for artists and writers for half a century. During a stroll into town one might have encountered Willem de Kooning, Conrad Marca-Relli, James Brooks, Robert Dash or Jackson Pollock's widow, Lee Krasner. The list of participants at annual shows at East Hampton's Guild Hall Museum read like a *Who's Who* of the New York art world. Although reclusive, Register felt that being near New York was important for his career. The future looked bright.

A Sense Of Mortality

In the spring and summer of 1980 John Register painted a number of strong pictures, including *Orange Storefront* (right), but he completed only two more canvases that year. He grew thin, and tired easily. At first he thought it was just too much running. Then his health deteriorated rapidly. What happened next would become the first of many battles to stay alive.

"In 1957, when I was 18, I was diagnosed as having a kidney disease called glomerulonephritis. At that time it was considered fatal. I was told it was like the fire in the basement of a house — you don't know it's there until it consumes you. I remember the doctor told me I would be lucky to live to 35. At the time dialysis was just being developed and there was no such thing as a kidney transplant — that was Buck Rogers stuff. I remember driving home from the doctor's office; I saw the sun dancing through the trees in a shimmering explosion of yellow color. I saw this one leaf almost electrified with sunlight, and it was the first time I had realized how beautiful things were. I'm sure I only realized it because I was going to die. I remember thinking, 'Jeez, these things are beautiful — and it's all going to be taken away when I die.' Of course, a week went by, and as I hadn't died yet, I stopped looking at the beauty of the green in the trees and went back to being a callow teen-ager."[1]

Now 41, Register suffered kidney failure. In a phone conversation with his sister Barbara, he was deeply touched when she offered one of her own kidneys for a transplant. In the fall of 1980, the Registers took a house in Santa Barbara, relatively near Los Angeles, in anticipation of John's transplant. Unable to clear toxins from his body by urination, he became dependent on three-times-a-week stints on a dialysis machine, an ordeal that made painting time much more precious.

"I painted some of my best pictures when I wasn't feeling well," said Register. "They're sometimes a little shaky. When I was feeling sick, I'd paint, lie down on

Orange Storefront, 1980
oil on canvas, 60 x 35 inches
Private Collection

Opposite:
Waiting Room for the Beyond,
1983
oil on canvas, 50 x 55 inches
Private Collection

Jamaica Avenue, 1980
oil on canvas, 50 x 50 inches
Collection of Mr. and Mrs. Peter Asher

the floor, get up and paint, lie on the floor again, and then get up to finish the picture. When you have a limited amount of energy, you tend not to overwork a painting. You're more lucid about what you have to say, less concerned with finish."[2]

Medical tests revealed that Barbara was a good tissue match, and the operation took place on January 22, 1981, at Cedars Sinai Hospital in Los Angeles. "There is no question that she saved my life," Register said. The transplant was a success, but he had to take steroids to calm the body's natural rejection process. The drugs caused him to gain weight, but they also gave him the energy to produce a number of important pictures.

That winter and spring he completed *Overpass near Rincon*, 1981 (below), near Rincon Point, a surf spot (glorified by the Beach Boys in "Surfin' U.S.A") just south of Santa Barbara. The underbelly of the freeway rips through what once was a peaceful ocean view. For compositional purposes, Register removed the Southern Pacific tracks as well as the telephone poles that appeared in his exploratory snapshots. In the spring of 1981, he had a one-man show at Malibu Art & Design and sold the larger paintings for $5,000 apiece.

In the summer, believing that the worst of John's health problems were behind them, the Registers returned to Long Island and rented a house at Springs, New York. Encouraged by Robert Dash, John began to paint country landscapes, generally in a small square format. Not surprisingly, the influences of Dash and Fairfield Porter crept into these pictures. "They were wristy little paintings."

Overpass Near Rincon, 1981
oil on canvas, 25 1/2 x 60 inches
Collection of Mr. and Mrs.
David B. McCall

said Register. "Being in the country I felt in touch with the weather and light patterns. I simplified my palette to three or four colors, but I would use 30 or 40 paintbrushes at a time. I would paint a few strokes and then drop the brush on the ground and grab a new one."[3]

The Registers moved to a new house in 1982 which had a painting studio overlooking a grassy field. John began surfing again and in the winter took up iceboat racing, known colloquially as "hard water sailing." Always competitive, he raced all over the Northeast, and participated in the North American Championships in 1983, but he also took time out to instruct his 14-year-old son David in the sport.

Health remained a concern. "You have to monitor a kidney carefully," Cathy recalled. "When we lived on Long Island, John would have to drive into Manhattan regularly. He was just one of many patients at a nephrology clinic at New York Hospital. He was shuffled around from doctor to doctor; they made mistake after mistake. He had a severe rejection episode that damaged the new kidney. Later they gave him the wrong medication, and he ended up in the hospital with bone marrow suppression and lost a dangerous amount of white blood cells."[4]

Despite setbacks that caused him depression and duress, his painting went well. Six important pictures came out of 1982, among them *Office* (opposite) and *Waiting Room* (p. 72). The inspiration for *Office* came when Register observed sunlight streaking across an office wall and highlighting a telephone sitting on a desk. The light projected the shadow of the telephone company's bell-shaped decal into a shadow that mimicked the real telephone on the desk. "The picture contains three symbols of communication," he wrote. "Normally, we can only look at an object from one point of view at a time. But because the decal on the window and its shadow on the wall occupy different planes than the three-dimensional phone, there is a suggestion of cubism."[5]

Telephones figured strongly in Register's personal iconography, notably in *Four Phone Booths*, 1974, *Phone by The Sea*, 1977, and *Mojave Bus Station*, 1978 (p. 71). Speaking

Study for 'Office,' 1982
Ink on paper, 11 x 14 inches
Private Collection

Opposite: *Office,* 1982
oil on canvas, 40 x 50 inches
Collection of John and
Barbara Martin/Black Sparrow
Press

Study for 'Two Telephones,' 1985
Ink on paper, 11 x 14 inches
Private collection

of *Two Telephones*, 1985 (below), he noted, "In some ways it's an ugly painting, but for me it was a successful painting. There's a telephone in one room and a telephone in another room — two instruments of communication and yet there is no communication. Just an air shaft apart, and yet the distance could be half a hemisphere. That's the way people are. It's hard to communicate, to get at the heart of somebody else. It's hard to get at the heart of me, too. I'm a difficult person to communicate with, even if I joke around. This painting is important — to understanding me."[6]

The Registers were voracious readers and their library was filled not only with classics but with the works of the artist-writer Wyndham Lewis and those of contemporary novelists such as Charles Bukowski and John Fante. It wasn't coincidence that more than 50 books on the Registers' shelf were

Two Telephones, 1985
oil on canvas, 30 x 48 1/2 inches
Estate of Pierre Prentki

Mojave Bus Station, 1978
oil on canvas,
28 1/2 x 39 1/2 inches
Collection of Mr. and Mrs.
W. Huston Lillard, III

Waiting Room, 1982
oil on canvas, 50 x 61 inches
Collection of Karen and
John Diefenbach

Opposite:
Yellow Couch, 1982
oil on canvas, 45 x 45 inches
Collection of Barbara and
Richard Mendelsohn

published by Black Sparrow Press. After an article about his work appeared in *Santa Barbara* magazine, in the summer of 1981, Register received his first fan letter: It was from John Martin, founder of Black Sparrow Press, then based in Santa Barbara. (Black Sparrow later moved to Santa Rosa.)

In 1965 Martin discovered the barroom poet Charles Bukowski, a literary unknown working for the post office. Sartre had not yet called Bukowski "America's greatest living poet," but Martin knew his whiskey-soaked verse was the real thing. That Bukowski was a brawling, womanizing drunk made little difference to the teetotaling Christian Scientist. Martin left the office supply business to start Black Sparrow Press specifically to publish this writer. He paid Bukowski $100 a month until he finished his first novel, *Post Office*, in 1969, and went on to publish some 40 of Bukowski's books of poetry and fiction. Martin also saw the potential in Register; eventually he bought four Register paintings, including *Office*.

Though years passed before Register and Martin met, they carried on a lively correspondence. Martin began sending Register regular packages of Black Sparrow books, among them Wyndham Lewis's *The Apes of God*, a 1930 novel satirizing artistic coteries. Register wrote Martin from East Hampton in September, 1981, that the novel had "parallels to the East Hampton art world, where everyone hates everyone else and so much vituperative dust is raised about nothing."[8]

Register had a romantic streak that was satisfied only through literature. In the winter of 1981-82, he read Herman Melville's *White Jacket*, which started him on a 19th-century sailing junket that included the Hornblower books, the Bounty series, *Moby-Dick*, most of Joseph Conrad and a biography of Lord Nelson. "I feel like I haven't touched land in two years," he wrote Martin. "I can't wait to get to . . . the Fante books."[9]

A protégé of H.L. Mencken, John Fante had been a novelist in the 1930s before turning to screenwriting for Hollywood. In 1980, Martin rediscovered the aging and blind Fante living in Malibu. He reprinted his forgotten novels as well as new works, including *Dreams From Bunker Hill* (1982). Fante, who died of complications from diabetes in 1983, was a great influence on Charles Bukowski — and on Register. The Fante novels featured the character Arturo Bandini, a young writer with grandiose dreams who was scratching out a life in Depression-era Hollywood. Register par-

Opposite:
View from the Train, 1982
oil on canvas, 36 1/2 x 45 inches
Collection of Jeffrey and
Valerie Peck

Brooklyn, 1982
oil on canvas, 50 x 50 inches
Private Collection

ticularly liked *Ask The Dust* (1939), which chronicles Bandini's seriocomic life in an old hotel in the Bunker Hill area of Los Angeles. After reading *Dreams From Bunker Hill* in March 1982, Register wrote Martin that the novel "made me nostalgic for the downtown L.A. area I frequented for subject matter."[10]

One of Register's paintings, *View of Palm*, 1985 (opposite), depicts late afternoon sunlight streaming though half-raised Venetian blinds, a palm tree barely visible though the smudged window glass. The pull cord dangles like a tiny hangman's noose. Register carefully noted in 1989 that there was no attempt at literary illustration, but for those who have read Fante's novels, it might well be the very window through which the impoverished Arturo Bandini crawls to avoid a confrontation with his landlady. Though their backgrounds were worlds apart, Register and Fante shared a similar view of Los Angeles. "Fante was a lonely sort of guy," Register said. "As a young man, he was always walking around fantasizing, looking for women in the same area that I was walking around fantasizing, looking for subject matter to paint."[11]

John Fante, author of *Ask The Dust*, circa 1939. His books influenced Register.

Opposite: *View of Palm*, 1985
oil on canvas, 50 x 50 inches
Collection of Martin Muller

By coincidence, Fante had been a close neighbor when the Registers first moved to their Bison Court house at Malibu, in 1973. They actually met briefly, yet neither man was aware of the other's identity. It happened on Halloween, 1975. "I was taking the kids out trick-or-treating around Point Dume; I thought I should get into the Halloween spirit," Register said. "I took one of those aluminum pushpins, ripped the pin off, and then glued it to my forehead. Then I took some alizarin crimson and painted blood tricking from it. Gruesomely subtle, I thought. Well we rang this guy's doorbell and John Fante came out to give the kids their candy. I was standing just inside the circle of light. Fante stared at me and his eyes focused and narrowed on that aluminum pushpin. Then, almost vehemently, he said, 'You ought to be ashamed of yourself.' I can't understand why he reacted so strongly to my pushpin. I didn't even know his name or that he was a writer until later. After he died, I happened to pick up one of his books, *West of Rome*, and as I read it, I found whole descriptions of our neighborhood and local events — like the time a dead whale washed up on the beach and stunk for days. Then I realized who he was."[12]

Long Island was a long way from those sunny California years, and Register was struggling with his painting. On July 20, 1982, he wrote John Martin, "The last year has been a difficult one for my painting... I have been frozen solid for the last month or so, unable to go in either direction, and then last week I did the *Office*. I framed it yesterday and I'm pleased with it. This is an emotion I haven't felt in a long time." He added: "I don't trust the opinions of dealers. I especially don't trust the opinions of other painters...and so, John, *your* correspondence has been very valuable to me."[13]

He enclosed a Polaroid of *Dining Car* (p. 80), a painting of a train interior begun in 1977 and reworked to completion in the winter of 1982. He also completed a similar picture, *View from the Train*, 1982 (p. 74).

Martin was impressed by the progress and wrote: "As a deeply interested on-looker, I can only urge you to follow the precise path laid out in your recent two oil paintings, *Dining Car* and *Office*. I will hope that no dealer, sensing possible profit, pushes you either in the direction of photo-realism or in the direction of decorative pastoral scenes."[14]

As Register was between dealers, John Martin recommended Martin Muller of Modernism Gallery in San Francisco.[15] Muller was an intense 29-year-old Swiss

Below left:
Uptown Downtown, 1983
oil on canvas, 35 x 50 inches
Collection of Brendan Ryan

Below right:
Long Island Expressway, 1983
oil on canvas, 18 x 24 inches
Private Collection

Southern Serves the South, 1983
oil on canvas, 50 x 70 inches
Collection of Mr. and Mrs.
Peter Trethewey

Dining Car, 1977–82
oil on canvas, 36 1/2 x 45 inches
Collection of George and Beth Gage

intellectual with a passion for Russian avant-garde art from 1910 to 1930 and for contemporary American art. In less than a decade, he had established a gallery known as one of the most adventurous in the Bay Area. (He was the first in San Francisco to show Kasemir Malevich, Andy Warhol, Robert Crumb, Mark Stock, Hermann Nitsch and Gottfried Helnwein.) Muller was also a fan of Bukowski's poetry and Fante's novels. Register's paintings struck him deeply, and he introduced Register in a one-man show in October, 1982.

San Francisco Chronicle art critic Thomas Albright, who had grown tired of the photo-realist movement prevalent at the time, begrudgingly praised Register's realism, noting the way light worked in Register's paintings, "subtly calling into question the reality of the things that it illuminates." Albright was at least partially mistaken in labeling Register a photo-realist, but offered this endorsement: "In the early days of photo-realism, the urban subject matter and aloof manner of most of its practitioners led to frequent comparisons with Edward Hopper. Register is one of the few whose work can stand up to that comparison."[16]

While 1982 was good for John's painting, it was not the best time for his health. In November Register wrote to John Martin: "I'm back in my studio for the first time in ten days... I've been associating myself with New York Hospital while they try and reverse a kidney rejection."[17]

In March 1983, Register wrote John Martin: "I'm finally off the painterly landscape binge. Must have something to do with the fact that I'm feeling much better. 'Landscape is the refuge of the ill.' That's my first aphorism.... I've been working on some large precisionist drawings of interiors with angles of light making patterns on the floor. The sky outside is like that seen from an airplane at 20,000 feet. Waiting rooms for the beyond. I hope the drawings result in a couple of big paintings."[18]

They did. *Waiting Room For the Beyond* (p. 64), painted in April, depicts a lone chair in a sun-filled room high up among the clouds. It is as if you have been summoned to the 200th floor of the Time, Life & Eternity Building. There is no receptionist, no one to greet you, but you know what that chair means.

Gerard Drive, 1983
oil on canvas, 50 x 50 inches
Collection of Adrian Keller

Life and death were very much on Register's mind and he did not suffer his illness passively. One day, after being told by a doctor that he had the flu, Register grew so desperate that he impersonated a physician over the phone so that he could obtain some lab results that had obviously been ignored. What he heard indicated he was having a major kidney-rejection episode. It was almost too late. "They put me into a ward with people who had hepatitis. There was blood on the floor. I thought at that point, 'I am going to die.'"[19]

Cathy wrote John Martin in November 1983 that because of mounting medical problems, she and her husband were considering moving to Los Angeles: "John is working on a large train interior which is colorful and exciting. I believe his heart is in the West."[20] She also enclosed a Polaroid of *Blue Chair* (below). That winter they made plans to leave the East Coast.

Blue Chair, 1984
oil on canvas, 50 x 70 inches
Collection of San Francisco
Museum of Modern Art

Opposite:
Curtain in the Wind, 1984
oil on canvas, 50 x 50 inches
Collection of Laguna Art Museum

The Return To The West

In the spring of 1984, the Registers returned to California to be near John's doctor, Stan Franklin. They bought a house on Latigo Canyon Road, high in the hills above Malibu. It was a Spanish-style house built in the 1920s. The elaborate gardens that once attracted busloads of horticultural enthusiasts had gone to seed. "The fountains have been cemented in and the shutters slam in the hot, dry wind," Register recalled. But it had privacy, a tennis court, and a view of the distant ocean. In spite of the rattlesnakes that regularly basked on the driveway and the coyotes that made off with their cat Pancho, it was perfect for the Registers. The nearest neighbor was a quarter mile away. "Just me, my wife, and the vultures up here," Register observed when I first interviewed him in 1986 for an article on Los Angeles artists.[1] Register was personable and charming, speaking warmly of his three children who were now away in boarding school and college. After the interview, he handily beat me in two sets of tennis.

In a small sunny studio to the right of the house, Register produced pictures with East Coast and West Coast imagery. *Cafe Winter*, 1984 (p. 87), was inspired by a restaurant in Passaic, New Jersey. *Midtown* (p. 93), with its rainy-day mood, came out of John's experiences in Manhattan. The other paintings of 1984, *Bus Station* (p. 86), *Southwest Motel* (p. 88) and *Cadillac Hotel* (p. 17), are interiors that could be anywhere in America, but the landscapes seen through the windows are clearly western.

On January 31, 1985, after three months of struggle, Register finished *View of Palm*. During the spring and summer of 1985, he made regular trips to a clinic for dialysis as he prepared for a second kidney transplant. He finished a major painting, *Restaurant By The Sea* (p. 89), which employed serial imagery in a surreal manner — dining tables that seem to go on forever. He also painted *Te Amo* (p. 90-91), a Manhattan

Purple Chair, 1987
oil on canvas, 70 x 50 inches
Collection of Paul and Cindy Levy

Opposite:
Road in The Desert, 1970
Photograph by John Register.

Bus Station, 1984
oil on canvas, 50 x 70 inches
Collection of J. Michael and
Marjorie A. Matthews

Opposite:
Cafe Winter, 1984
oil on canvas, 50 x 50 inches
Collection of Joan Preston O'Neil

street scene near an elevated subway platform. The title refers not to an affection for Spanish Harlem but to a display ad for a brand of Mexican-made cigars.

One day Register returned home from playing chess at a friend's and was given good news. "My son Peter looked up from his newspaper and said, 'Oh, by the way, someone called from the hospital. They've got a kidney for you.' It happened on Cathy's birthday, August 11." The kidney came from a woman killed in a car accident in Florida. The organ was shipped by air to Los Angeles in a red-and-white Igloo picnic cooler. He entered Cedars Sinai Hospital that night to be prepped. The doctors cross-matched blood and tissue samples, and the results were good. They went into the operating room the next morning.

Register's friend and chess partner, Dr. James Forrester, who was then head of cardiac research at Cedars Sinai, wanted to attend the operation. "I had an epidural spinal so I was wide-awake, and Jim and I chatted away while they were operating," Register said. "I said, 'Jim, do you feel like playing a little chess?' and

Study for 'Restaurant by the Sea,' 1985
ink and colored pencil on paper,
14 x 17 inches
Collection of Catherine Register

Restaurant by the Sea, 1985
oil on canvas, 50 x 70 inches
Private Collection

Opposite:
Southwest Motel, 1984
oil on canvas, 50 x 50 inches
Collection of Barnaby Conrad III

Los Angeles, 1985
oil on canvas, 50 x 70 inches
Collection of John and
Susan Caldwell

Previous pages:
Te Amo, 1985
oil on canvas, 50 x 91 inches
Collection of Bob and Diane Pryt

he said, 'Sure, that'd be great.' So I said 'Pawn to king-four,' and he said 'Pawn to queen bishop-three,' and I said, 'Pawn to queen-four,' and so on. We were 17 moves into the classical variation of Caro-Kahn when Dr. Cohen, the surgeon, distracted with our laughter, gave me a little something that didn't quite knock me out but it made me drowsy enough that I lost the thread of our game. I still kid Forrester that it's one of the few games he's ever won off me." (Register later added, "That's not really true, because Jim has a United Chess Federation rating over 2,000.")[2]

Two weeks later, Register was fit enough to fly up to San Francisco for his second one-man show at Modernism. The gallery and Black Sparrow Press had just issued a small catalog of his work, with text by Jeffrey Browning. *San Francisco Chronicle* art critic Kenneth Baker gave Register a solid review: "The ingenuity of Register's paintings is his ability to find the most economical color equivalents possible for effects of light and atmosphere. He has a knack for describing the light secreted in shadows." Baker commented particularly on *Los Angeles* (p.

Midtown, 1984
oil on canvas, 50 x 60 inches
Private Collection

Long Island Expressway Toll Gate, 1984
oil on canvas, 30 x 50 inches
Collection of Lloyd B. Erikson

92), saying, "I have never seen a painting that captures the peculiar ominousness of L.A. better than this one."3

In the next few years, Register's health stabilized and he resumed a full life of hard work. In tennis games with friends his aggressive serve made him a formidable opponent. There were also family backpacking adventures in the Wind River region of Wyoming and surfing trips to Hawaii. He continued taking steroids and immunosuppressives to keep his body from rejecting the foreign kidney. The drugs made him prone to skin cancers, which were removed. He soon bore the weathered look of a sun-wrecked mariner. He was also more susceptible to common illnesses and tried to avoid crowded movie theaters and airplanes. His health concerns led to somber glimpses of mortality in his paintings.

After the transplant Register's energy rose and he painted one big picture almost every month. Five were restaurant interiors, among them *Desert Restaurant*, 1986 (opposite). In this picture of a road stop cafe, a row of glinting bar stools draws the viewer's eye into the cool blue interior, and then to the hot orange desert landscape framed in the windows. The interior was based on an urban restaurant that Register photographed in Passaic, New Jersey, near the town's waterfalls. Instead of water flowing outside, he substituted a scene that could be in New Mexico or Arizona. "It's not so much East [Coast] versus West Coast. I like desert imagery and the stillness it implies…. In *Desert Restaurant* I wanted to show the difference between the shelter inside and the unforgiving desert outside. You can die in the desert. A cafe is refuge. In *Desert Restaurant*, the viewer sees a safe environment, while outside is an environment that would kill him."4

Unlike trendier L.A. artists, Register never associated with the art crowd of Venice, a scene then taking on some of the glitzier aspects of nearby Hollywood. A successful L.A. artist in the 1980s was more likely to be considered a celebrity than an intellectual. "I don't mind seeing a few friends, but I hate art openings, even my own," said Register. "Talking about art with other artists has never been productive for me. I just figure that what's in me is what I have to deal with."5 He continued to build on themes and subject matter from the early years of his painting career, but now the paint-handling revealed an artist in complete control of his vision — or perhaps a complete inner vision in control of a painter.

Opposite:
Desert Restaurant, 1986
oil on canvas, 50 x 70 inches
Collection of Art Kern

Study for 'Desert Restaurant,'
1986
oil on paper, 16 x 20 inches
Collection of Catherine Register

Office Chairs, 1985
oil on canvas, 50 x 70 inches
Collection of Jeffrey and
Evelyne Thomas

Register had his favorite artists, and they weren't who one might expect. He owned two photographs by Henri-Cartier Bresson and a watercolor by Charles Burchfield. Of Eric Fischl he wrote in 1989, "I like the social commentary and the sexual violence in his imagery. He's a wonderful painter. Completely unrelated to my own work, an artist I admire is Chaim Soutine…. What I found marvelous about Richard Diebenkorn in his figurative period was his surface, his paint handling. I love paint! Charles Burchfield's retrospective at the Metropolitan Museum a few years ago was, in my opinion, one of the great shows of all time. I also admire Anselm Kiefer. I wish I could portray American greed with the intensity that Kiefer did Germany's Nazism. The paintings are so organic, they look like God made them."[6]

In 1986, the Francis J. Greenburger Foundation selected Register and four other artists for an award given to artists "of extraordinary merit who have not yet achieved wide public recognition." The jury consisted of Guggenheim director Tom Messer, artist Robert Motherwell, critic Clement Greenburg, dealer André

Lobby, 1985
oil on canvas, 50 x 70 inches
Collection of Robert and
Jane Kantor

Mojave Desert, 1986
oil on canvas, 50 x 70 inches
Collection of Francis J. Greenburger

Diner with Red Seats, 1986
oil on canvas, 50 x 50 inches
Private Collection

Mustard Jar, 1987
oil on canvas, 50 x 70 inches
Collection of Paul and
Linda Fusco

Opposite:
Silver Lake Restaurant, 1987
oil on canvas, 50 x 70 inches
Collection of Timothy Pratt

Following pages:
Nebraska, 1987
oil on canvas, 40 x 90 inches
Collection of Bernie Brillstein

Emmerich, and collector Eloise Spaeth. Lillian Ross wrote an account of the awards banquet for *The New Yorker*.⁷

In 1988, John Martin asked Register to design the cover of Charles Bukowski's new novel, *Hollywood*, which ribaldly described his experiences in Tinseltown during the filming of his autobiographical film *Barfly* (starring Faye Dunaway and Mickey Rourke). Though the artist had long since given up illustration, he admired Bukowski's writing enough to turn out a watercolor of a neon martini glass tilting over the famed Hollywood sign at dusk.

Register's health remained steady after the second transplant, and on several occasions from 1987 to 1989 he and Cathy traveled the country in search of imagery. One of the more unsettling pictures is *Mojave Couple*, 1987 (p. 106-107). Compositionally it is an exquisite balance of diagonals that zigzag back into the picture, but the mood suggests a seedy Bukowski story: The lower-middle-class cottage is characterless, we're not sure we really want to know who the half-naked woman and fleshy, beer-drinking man are, and the wary mongrel does not encourage us to pry. Register said the painting was inspired by Manet's once-scandalous work *Dejeuner sur l'herbe*, 1862, but also acknowledged his affinity for Eric Fischl's work. "Driving through the town of Mojave, I was struck in passing by the image of this couple, and asked if they would mind if I took a few photographs. 'What is this for?' they asked. 'I'm a painter,' I said. 'I'm trying to make sense out of life.' I'm sure they thought I was mad. Nevertheless, they gave me a beer."⁸

A lonely human figure appears in *Man Seated in a Restaurant*, 1987 (opposite). Register found this scene along the Pacific Coast Highway, near Malibu. "Across the aisle was a man waiting for his food. Perhaps he was just pondering the arrival of 'The Catch of the Day,' but I saw Rodin's *Thinker*. I made a detailed drawing of him on my paper table mat. But when I got back to my studio and tried to make up the rest of the interior, I found it impossible. I castigated myself for being unable to re-create a simple room. So I returned to the restaurant in the late afternoon a few days later and made enough photographs so that I could finish the painting."⁹

Study for 'Man seated in Restaurant,' 1986
ink on paper, 14 1/2 x 15 1/2 inches
Courtesy of Modernism Gallery, San Francisco

Opposite:
Man Seated in Restaurant, 1987
oil on canvas, 50 x 50 inches
Private Collection

Though Register's paintings have a deliberate, almost *destined* look to them, their conception largely relied on the accidental. *Suits*, 1988 (opposite), is a good example. "I was called for jury duty downtown," he recalled. "Unlike a lot of my friends who are self-employed, I didn't try to be excused, even though it meant giving up 10 days of my life. I found the experience fascinating. One day as I was walking downtown, I saw this shop window with men's suits displayed on 12 headless dummies. It occurred to me that we, the jury, must have looked that way to the defendant."[10] There is also an echo of Hollywood slang, wherein accountants and lawyers are derogatorily referred to as "suits."[11]

The search for subject matter gradually took the artist farther afield. His preferred method of travel was by train. In June of 1988 the Registers lived in a rented house in Paseo Canyon while remodeling their new house at Malibu. "The three children all had house guests, the phone was ringing around the clock, and the

Storefront, 1987
oil on canvas, 40 x 49 inches
Courtesy of Modernism Gallery,
San Francisco

Previous pages:
Mojave Couple, 1987
oil on canvas, 40 x 90 inches
Collection of Mr. and Mrs.
Duncan A. Chapman

Suits, 1988
oil on canvas, 50 x 70 inches
Collection of Bernie Brillstein

Last of the Old City, 1988
oil on canvas, 35 x 50 inches
Collection of Emilio Estevez

television was blaring.... I said to Cathy: 'I have to get out of here.' She knows when I'm really desperate. So she phoned Amtrak and told the man, 'My husband doesn't care where he goes, he just wants to be away for two weeks on a train.' The idea of having no destination somehow appealed to the guy on the other end of the line. He understood the idea of a trip without a destination, without a real purpose."

Register was routed from Los Angeles to Las Vegas to Salt Lake City to Denver to Chicago. The return took him across the Midwest with stops at Whitefish, Montana, then Seattle, Portland, and home. "I had a bag that doubled as a suitcase and backpack. I stayed in old hotels near the train stations. I would get up at 5 in the morning when the light was soft and no one was around. The idea was to have no preconceptions about paintings, but I hoped to see something significant which I would then photograph. I would work until about 9 or 10 and have some breakfast in a cafe. When the late afternoon brought interesting shadows,

Lost Bus, 1989
oil on canvas, 49 x 72 inches
Private Collection

Fast Food, 1987
oil on canvas, 35 x 50 inches
Collection of Lili and Ambrose Monell

Backyard, 1988
oil on canvas, 35 x 50 inches
Collection of Peter and
Karen Register

I headed out into the streets again until dark. It's like a vacation from all concerns. Zen people go to a retreat to contemplate things. Well, this is what I meditate on, trains and cities."[12]

A good part of the trip for Register was spent observing different levels of American life. In a postcard sent to his dealer, Martin Muller, he wrote: "The train offers strange glimpses. A construction worker trying to take a solitary leak behind a building. A topless, bare-breasted girl wading in a shallow river framed by yellow-green river bank trees. She brazenly faced the windows. Walked to the lounge car at 5:00 A.M. Travelers all looked pole-axed by nerve gas. Mouths agape. Rosy dawn in the distance."[13]

In *Watching the Storm (Denver)*, 1988 (p. 6-7), Register split the canvas diagonally into exterior and interior, complex and simple, near and distant. Even the light is divided: There is strong sunlight on the chair, but outside, framed by the window, a storm moves in over Denver's skyline. The tunnel-like painting called *The Loop*, 1988 (p. 116), was inspired by Register's two-day visit to Chicago.[14] A stop on the return trip produced the stunning *The Counter*, 1988 (opposite), whose power comes from the luscious brushstrokes in the rendering of the counter's reflective surface.

The rail odyssey also produced *Train Interior* (p. 118), a frontal composition abstracted by sunlight into triangles and rectangles of color. "There's something fascinating about being on a train — you're traveling, but you're going nowhere," said the artist. "You sit in a compartment but you're hurtling along at 80 miles an hour. I tried to give the painting a sense of stillness."[15]

In mid-January, 1989 I interviewed Register for three days to produce the first monograph on his work (Chronicle Books, 1989). Although he was eager to assist in cataloging pictures for the book, he was by turns open and reticent when it came to speaking about his painting motifs. He loosened up in the evening over a rum and tonic, yet he never let me into his studio while he was painting.

The moody cityscape *Chicago*, 1989 (p. 117), stood on the artist's easel while a black-and-white oil sketch for it hung over his fireplace. "I knew there was something wrong with the picture," he told me. "Usually I start a painting with a thumbnail drawing either done from life or from a photograph, then a color sketch

Portrait of Martin Muller, 1988
oil on canvas, 17 1/2 x 17 1/2 inches
Collection of Martin Muller

Opposite:
The Counter, 1988
oil on canvas, 50 x 50 inches
Collection of Garen and
Sharalyn King Staglin

Self-portrait on a Train, 1986
ink on postcard, 3 1/2 x 5 1/2 inches
Collection of Barnaby Conrad III

in oils. The thing is, if you solve all the problems in the sketch, it takes away the desire to do the picture on a larger scale. But of course scale changes everything. Now it's harder to move things around. You can lose the vitality of the sketch."

The central image of this painting was an old hotel. "It's pretty rundown and just a step away from being bulldozed. Which I find fascinating. Maybe it's just because I feel I'm one step away from being bulldozed myself. I pushed every building around that hotel back into the atmosphere, into the distance. I suppose there's a metaphor there — the isolated person in a crowd."[16]

Register explained in writing his painting technique. Using a color or black-and-white photograph as a primary source, "I draw a basic outline of the elements with a blue pencil on the canvas. If there are signs (i.e., lettering) or some other difficult-to-render elements I project them and outline them in blue pencil on the canvas. I underpaint with the cool colors yellow ochre, alizarin crimson, and ultramarine blue. These are cool colors. I block in the painting by concentrating on lights and darks, the masses, and not worrying about the color until later. I move some elements around, or take them out, or put stuff in. I spend a lot of time just mixing to get what I think is the right color. I often use five or six

The Loop, 1988
oil on canvas, 50 x 70 inches
Collection of Bronson, Bronson & McKinnon

Opposite:
Chicago, 1989
oil on canvas, 50 x 70 inches
Collection of Mr. and Mrs. Eric Lieber

Train Interior, 1988
oil on canvas, 50 x 70 inches
Private Collection

gray paper palettes at once. One palette for the sky, one palette for the trees, one palette for the building, et cetera."[17] It generally took him four to eight weeks to finish a large painting.

Register liked to take an almost-finished painting out of the studio and hang it on the living room wall. "That way I can look at it at different times of the day. You can live with the picture. See its strengths and weaknesses. I also use the children's eyes and Cathy's to try to see it differently. Cathy is my most important critic. I couldn't paint without her."[18]

Since he often spent weeks, even months, on the same picture, Register found it hard at times to sustain a single mood throughout the process. "I may start the painting in bright, high-key colors and then gradually knock the picture down. A week later, the colors may brighten again depending on what works and how I feel."[19]

One of Register's pet peeves was art criticism that he called "art babble," and he found most art magazines unreadable. While he admired some abstract painting, his interest lay in figurative work. "For me, realism is more than just making a chair look like a chair. People say realism is mindless. The art magazines say that, dismissing it. I just don't see that. They're never going to get rid of realism. There will be different art movements but there will always be a straight-on line of realists who use the elements of reality to make it add up to something — to something more."[20]

In early 1989, John and Cathy took a road trip through Texas, but it seemed harder and harder for him to see "something more" in the jarring commercial strips he found in the small towns. Within a week after returning, however, he began painting from a photo of an El Paso restaurant. Chairs that were originally vermilion were painted a cool red. Outside the window of the landlocked restaurant, he brushed in a cold blue ocean whose surface was barely riffled by swells, and the picture became *Pacific Rim Restaurant*, 1989 (p. 23). He wrote me in March to say he had finished the painting, adding a paragraph that seemed to speak of more than just his approach to art: "Every painting starts as pure vision. Every brushstroke leads you further away from the vision. At the end, if the vision is barely discernible, you have to be grateful."[21]

Reno, 1988
oil on canvas, 50 x 35 inches
Private Collection

Late Years

On August 10, 1989, Register went into Cedars Sinai Hospital, where surgeons discovered he had cancerous cells in the lymph nodes of his groin. A big decision had to be made. He could stay on the immunosuppressive drugs and risk cancer, or go off them and risk losing the kidney. Register said he would rather face cancer. He wrote his mother, "I've had a lot of practice dealing with these sort of problems. I am by nature positive and belligerent, two characteristics that work well not only on the medical profession but on my psyche."[1]

That fall John executed a crisp silk-screen print of the neon martini and Hollywood sign that had first appeared on the cover of Charles Bukowski's novel.[2] On October 14 John Martin, dealer Martin Muller and Register met at the author's house in San Pedro. Register recalled that "Hank," as Bukowski was known to his friends, was not at all the brawler and fight picker he'd imagined. As writer and artist co-signed the prints, Bukowski ribbed Register good-naturedly, calling him "the only artist I ever met who isn't an asshole." Though an admirer of his paintings, Bukowski told him, "You'd be a better painter if you'd had a miserable childhood." Despite these prods from the older man, Bukowski and Register took to each other. "I found him to be a sweet, gentle guy with a great sense of humor," Register recalled. "He was on a wine wagon, so maybe that's why I didn't get the version I've read about.... If I were to define my kinship with Bukowski it's that we share a wary eye for humanity and a love for solitude."[3] Register regretted that they weren't able to spend more time together, but both men were facing health problems.

The first major monograph on John Register was published by Chronicle Books in 1989 with a text by this author. Martin Muller celebrated the publication with a black-tie dinner for 100 guests at Bix Restaurant in San Francisco. John resisted the fancy doings at first, but he was proud of the book and ended up enjoying

Register and Bukowski co-signing the print *Hollywood*, 1989, with Martin Muller.

Opposite:
Wasteland Hotel, 1989
oil on canvas, 49 x 70 inches
Collection of Tom Patchett,
Los Angeles

Hollywood, 1989
Silk-screen, 21 x 17 inches
Edition of 75.
Courtesy of Modernism
Gallery, San Francisco

himself at the party.[4] He had much to celebrate. The year 1989 was one of his most productive, with 14 major paintings leaving the studio, among them *Interstate Cafe* (opposite), *Bunker Hill* (p. 2-3), *Bakersfield* (below), *Desert Diner* (p. 125) and the haunting interior *Wasteland Hotel* (p. 120).

In February, John wrote about the prospect of exhibiting in New York: "I'm ambivalent about New York. Maybe my testosterone is ebbing. Martin [Muller] does a good job, he is honest, and he doesn't pressure me. Also, I think there is a certain integrity in being a regionalist, a California painter.... I'm not mentally suited to painting shows. I make paintings one at a time, I agonize over them, I destroy a number of them.... Maybe because Martin is a European-style dealer.... he respects my work habits."[5]

Bakersfield, 1989
oil on canvas, 35 x 50 inches
Collection of Martin Muller

Opposite:
Interstate Cafe, 1989
oil on canvas, 50 x 70 inches
Private Collection

Ventura Freeway, 1989
oil on canvas, 49 x 72 inches
Private Collection

Desert Diner, 1989
oil on canvas, 65 x 49 inches
Collection of Paul and
Linda Fusco

Leaving L.A. on the Desert Wind,
1989–91
oil on canvas, 40 x 90 inches
Collection of Dr. James Forrester
and Dr. Barbara Bick

Hotel in Desert, 1991
oil on canvas, 35 x 50 inches
Collection of Richard and Angie Thieriot

Train Compartment, 1990
oil on canvas, 70 x 49 inches
Collection of Frederick and
Nina Carroll

The Interrogation, 1990–91
oil on canvas, 50 x 70 inches
Collection of Olivier Weber-Caflisch

Texas Cafe, 1989
oil on canvas, 50 x 70 inches
Private Collection

Motel: Route 66, 1991
oil on canvas, 35 x 50 inches
Collection of John Kimball

Waiting at the Terminal (Airport), 1990-91
oil on canvas, 70 x 49 inches
Collection of Mr. and Mrs. Michael S. Engl

Register had always been drawn to Northern California and decided to spend the winter and spring of 1990 in Oakland making prints at Magnolia Editions. He executed a color lithograph after the painting *Pacific Rim Restaurant*, as well as etchings inspired by the painting *Cadillac Hotel*, a number of which he had Cathy watercolor over. At the urging of Black Sparrow publisher John Martin, Register also created a suite of six black-and-white etchings to accompany the previously unpublished prologue to John Fante's novel *Ask The Dust*. The prologue is a young man's poetic meditation on love, life and loss. Register responded with a light-struck cityscape of the young Fante wandering through the Bunker Hill area of Los Angeles, as well as some moody interiors of rooming houses. (These would later serve as sketches for major paintings at the end of Register's life).[6]

In Santa Monica Register also produced two large silk-screens, after the paintings *Venetian Light* (p. 12) and *Wasteland Hotel*, that were ambitious in scale and masterly in execution.[7] These and other works on paper were exhibited at Modernism Gallery in September, 1990.

Two months later Register underwent surgery for skin cancer on his right hand, followed a week later by a second cataract operation. Though an unpleasant procedure, it cleared up his eyesight and he painted at full throttle. His health was stable and 16 paintings left the studio in 1991. One of his most personal pictures was *The Swimmer*, 1991 (opposite), which depicted a man struggling against the tides at the base of a sea cliff; an almost spiritual light spills from a cavern in the rocks. The cliffs were inspired by Big Sur, but the model for the swimmer was son Peter, who shivered in the wintry water off Westward Beach while Register photographed him. John wrote to me: "Blake did a painting of what you were to see when you died. This is something that interests me. The ocean is the primordial ooze from which we ascended. For my version of the death experience I have man returning to the ocean ooze and heading towards the beautiful light."[8]

He also painted *Rooming House*, 1991 (p. 136), a square canvas of a brooding man cloistered in darkened rooms; the setting is clearly Los Angeles, as the image first appeared among the etchings illustrating the Fante prologue. Indeed, an early title for it was *Fante at the Typewriter*.

The Swimmer, 1991
oil on canvas, 50 x 70 inches
Collection of Michael G. Klein

Study for 'The Window of Opportunity,' 1990
gouache on paper,
dimensions unknown
Private collection

Opposite:
The Window of Opportunity,
1990–91
oil on canvas, 50 x 70 inches
Collection of Mr. and Mrs.
Brad Grey

In May 1992, Register began painting a street scene in Manhattan. He wrote his friend Eugene Beck, "I truly have no idea where it is taking me. Yesterday I knocked back all the details with a glaze of ultramarine and raw sienna. It's of Times Square in New York. I'd like to superimpose a neon sign advertising pornography over the glaze."[9] The picture became *Times Square* (p. 138-139). Instead of the neon porno sign, John introduced a slightly balding man in a dark suit stepping off the left-hand curb — his quick-striding art dealer, Martin Muller.

Few post-World War II American artists have recorded major political events in their art. While it was also unusual for Register, he believed his paintings should evoke not only what a place looked like but how its inhabitants felt at that time. "I want people to see my paintings years from now and get a good — as in accurate — feeling for the way it was."[10] In 1992 South Los Angeles was torn apart by riots after several police officers were acquitted in the infamous Rodney King case. (An amateur's videotape had captured the police clubbing King, an African American, with their batons during his arrest in 1991.) Register's response to this

Winona Motel, 1990
oil on canvas, 50 x 35 inches
Collection of Lili and
Ambrose Monell

Mesa Cafe, 1991
oil on canvas, 50 x 70 inches
Collection of Peter E. Thieriot

Opposite:
Rooming House, 1991
oil on canvas, 50 x 50 inches
Courtesy of Modernism Gallery,
San Francisco

Following pages:
Detail of *Times Square*, 1993
oil on canvas, 50 x 90 inches
Collection of Frederick and
Nina Carroll

Houses Near Freeway, 1991
oil on canvas, 35 x 50 inches
Collection of David and
Victoria Register

Opposite:
Oakland, 1991
oil on canvas, 50 x 40 inches
Collection of Elizabeth M. Gordon

The Conversation, 1991
oil on canvas, 50 x 70 inches
Collection of Richard Segal

Curtains in the Wind, 1991
oil on canvas, 50 x 70 inches
Collection of Bob and
Pat Eggers

Frankie & Johnny, 1992
oil on canvas, 35 x 50 inches
Collection of Penny and
Noel Nellis

Opposite:
La Brea Motel, 1992
oil on canvas, 35 x 50 inches
Private Collection

Fresno, 1991
oil on canvas, 50 x 90 inches
Private Collection

The Journey, 1992
oil on canvas, 35 x 50 inches
Courtesy of Modernism
Gallery, San Francisco

Opposite:
Man in Reflected Light, 1992
oil on canvas, 50 x 40 inches
Collection of Emilio Estevez

L.A. at Dawn, 1993
oil on canvas, 50 x 90 inches
Collection of Les and
Ginger Crane

Two Red Stools, 1993
oil on canvas, 35 x 50 inches
Collection of Chuck and
Becky Daggs

Gallup Still Life, 1993
oil on canvas, 35 x 50 inches
Private Collection

Hotel by Railroad, 1993
oil on canvas, 35 x 50 inches
Collection of Catherine Register

Late Afternoon Light, 1994–95
oil on canvas, 40 x 50 inches
Collection of Rick and
Dana Dirickson

Three Tables, 1993
oil on canvas, 50 X 50 inches
Private Collection

Lunch, 1993
oil on canvas, 50 x 35 inches
Private Collection

conflagration was a disturbing picture called *L.A. Riots*, 1993 (opposite), which depicts a suburban couple oblivious to the flames and smoke billowing on the horizon. The models for the couple were Cathy's brother and sister-in-law, who had just visited from Vermont; the pool-side setting was the Registers' house in Malibu.

The Earl McGrath Gallery of L.A. showed Register's work in April, 1993. Concurrently, a retrospective curated by Jeffrey Herr opened at the Los Angeles Municipal Art Gallery. In his comments in the catalog, Herr astutely observed that while Register's "existentialist outlook presents a certain pessimism regarding man's stewardship over his domain, there is a human perspective which permits the possibility of at least partial redemption."[11]

In July, Cathy and John drove through the Southwest and up to Idaho. They flew to the remote Selway Lodge in Idaho and rode horses up to a small mountain lake, fishing by day and drinking red wine under the stars. Though weak,

Burrito, 1992
oil on canvas, 33 x 50 inches
Collection of Frederick Hill

Opposite:
L.A. Riots, 1993
oil on canvas, 63 x 50 inches
Private Collection

The Colorado, 1995
oil on canvas, 50 x 70 inches
Collection of Chuck
and Becky Daggs

John insisted on backpacking down the mountain. It was to be his last outdoor adventure, but the road trip yielded material to paint *The Colorado* (opposite), a shadowy self-portrait set in a darkened coffee shop.

After Charles Bukowski's death in 1994, Register pulled out photos of the writer and painted a portrait of him in April. In a letter to his mother Register wrote: "I am struggling with the posthumous portrait of Charles Bukowski. He has a wonderful beaten-up face from all his bar room fights, and life in general. Craters from childhood acne, warts on his eye lids, and a nose that's been compared to a Studebaker hood with Buick fenders for nostrils. A great face to paint."[12]

In the summer of 1994, Register agreed to do a painting for *The Martini*, my book about the classic cocktail. (Ed Ruscha, Mel Ramos, Gottfried Helnwein, Guy Diehl and Mark Stock also contributed works.) Originally John intended to paint himself as an over-the-hill 50-year-old man in a time of tragedy. He enlisted his son Peter, a professional photographer, to shoot the scene, but then picked up the camera himself. "Halfway through the shoot I thought it would be an interesting twist, something not quite so predictable, to have the failure be a young man's failure," John said. "He's drinking his father's or grandfather's drink, implying a belief in tradition, and obviously if he's drinking in the middle of the day, a tradition that has failed him....the Old Boy network, the prep school, Ivy League, country-club, debutante-party tradition is played out, or at least that's what the painting is trying to say."[13]

The result was the sardonic *Martini*, 1994 (p. 164). Register was careful to say that this was in no way a portrait of his son Peter, who had never even consumed a martini. Working on the picture, however, seemed to stir up memories of his own childhood. "When I was young and rebellious, I rejected the martini and all it stood for," he wrote me. "Now I like to drink them. My fondest memory of the martini relates to my stepfather. When dinner would be served, he would toss the undrunk portion of his martini into the fireplace. There would be a pyrotechnic *whoof* off the eucalyptus logs, and we children would marvel at the jet fuel that propelled our parents."[14]

In the fall of 1994, it became apparent that the skin cancers on Register's scalp were not responding to heavy radiation treatments. On September 7, a 2-inch

Bukowski, 1994
oil on canvas, 20 x 16 inches
Collection of John and
Barbara Martin/Black
Sparrow Press

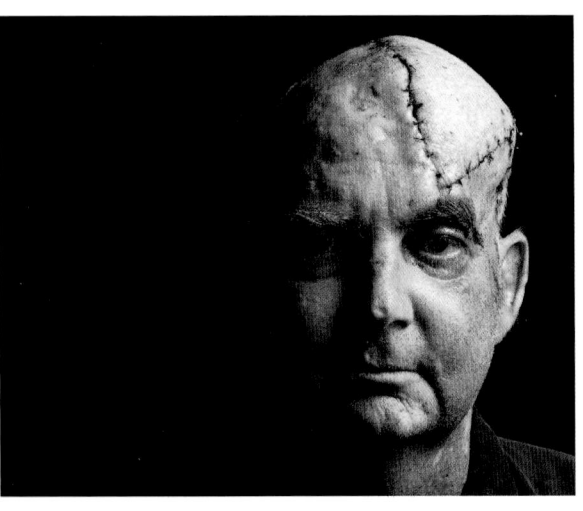

Register after surgery in 1994. He signed the photo, "With love from the abyss." Photograph by Peter Register.

Opposite:
Vacancy, 1994
oil on canvas, 40 x 50 inches
Collection of Kathryn Register

square hole was cut out of his skull and replaced with a bone graft; fully one-half of his scalp was removed and replaced with an 8-inch-long slab of skin and flesh cut from below his shoulder blade. The surgery took almost 14 hours and involved a half-dozen surgeons. His entire family and many friends donated blood. A few days later, in a tricky operation, the surgeon removed a cancerous nerve in the eye socket that was just 1 centimeter away from the brain. The operation was a success, but it left Register horribly scarred.

Two months later a chest scan revealed that the skin cancers had metastasized and there were lesions in both lungs. The doctors did not give him long to live. It was a terrible blow to Register and his family, but within days he was painting again. In late October he finished the picture *Vacancy*, 1994 (opposite). This painting was inspired by an empty pool Register had photographed at the Big Pillow Motel in Wells, Nevada, on his last road trip through the Southwest. Compared to *Mojave Pool*, of 1976, it is dark and autumnal.

One day an eccentric octogenarian cousin of the Registers named Leila Sherman stopped by the house and questioned him about the picture, a conversation John recorded in a letter to his mother:

There was a large new painting on the wall behind me at the dining room table. I saw Leila trying to focus on it. 'Is that a swimming pool?' she asked.
'It's an empty pool with rocks in it.'
'What is that building back there?'
'It's an abandoned motel and you can see in the sky a storm is coming.'
'And that's a pay phone?'
'Yes, but it's a special phone; it only takes money, it doesn't give it back, and there are no buttons so you can't make calls; you can only receive them, but you might have to wait awhile before you get called.'
'How dreadful. Where did you find something like that?'
'In my mind.'

Leila Sherman left shaken, and later told another relative that John's paintings were "godless," which amused the artist.[15]

Martini, 1994
oil on canvas, 50 x 35 inches
Collection of Suzanne and
Guy Lampard

In early November, the Registers' black Labrador Lola was put to sleep at the house. The event planted a deep sorrow in John. "It was so final. Fourteen years of unqualified love."[16] Cathy later said that witnessing this beloved pet's death made John decide against any kind of medically assisted suicide for himself.

Register was not particularly religious, saying to a friend that he was missing the "God gene," but he also once called himself "an existential Christian."[17] For almost four decades he had enjoyed a long-distance friendship with Robert S. Morse, a traditional Episcopal Bishop who had been the chaplain at UC Berkeley when Register was a student. In a spontaneous act of generosity, Register pulled the painting *Big Brother* off the wall of his second show and gave it to the priest. Bishop Morse flew down to spend a few hours with the artist that he had always remembered as "a remarkable young man." Register wrote him, "Your blessing was a very moving experience. I'd been feeling kind of closed down. I'm not even sure of the words you said, but I did, somewhere in the middle of the blessing feel a great release. It is as though the heavens opened up."[18]

To boost Register's spirits, Martin Muller called and insisted the artist paint a show for September, 1995. Register wrote his friends George and Beth Gage: "I think I will do it if only because it will give me an incentive to work harder. It will just be in the front room [of Modernism] so if I get moving I could do four big paintings between now and then and save my soul."[19]

Throughout January, 1995, Register was fatigued by radiation treatment, but he worked constantly. A large part of his strength came from Cathy. "Without her constant attention and encouragement," Peter Register told me, "Dad wouldn't have been able to paint, much less survive. She did everything for him." On February 4 Register finished the painting of Cathy titled *Woman by the Sea* (p. 168). It had been over two decades since he first painted her in a pink bikini as *Girl on the Chaise*, 1973 (p. 41). The next day he began another large picture, *Two Telephones* (p. 169). Though there were walks on the beach, his spirits were up and down and the chest pains and headaches continued. In March he began a small still life of objects in his studio.

Drowning in Hollywood, 1995
oil on canvas, 22 x 32 inches
Collection of Scott A. Stone

165

Twin Arrows Cafe, 1994
oil on canvas, 22 x 28 inches
Collection of Larry
and Joan Evans

Desert Gas Station, 1994
oil on canvas, 40 x 50 inches
Collection of Garen and
Sharalyn King Staglin

On March 22 Register's oncologist, Dr. John Glaspy, noted that the tumor in John's chest was 100 percent larger. His nephrologist, Dr. Gabriel Danovitch, concluded that the only option left was to take him off all immunosuppressant drugs. Register agreed, and celebrated the decision by working on another small still life and taking a walk on the beach. He completed the still life on April 15, spent the evening coughing up blood, but two days later started another picture, *Drowning in Hollywood* (p. 165). The model for the picture was Lex Sidon, a friend of his son Peter. The painting struck Cathy as "very sad" because the dark-haired man closely resembled the young John Register in his advertising days. Register attempted a larger version but put it aside to start, *The Motel By The Freeway* (p. 178).[20]

Woman by the Sea, 1995
oil on canvas, 35 x 50 inches
Private Collection

Two Telephones, 1995
oil on canvas, 35 x 50 inches
Courtesy of Modernism
Gallery, San Francisco

Going Towards The Vanishing Point

On the morning of May 8, 1995, John Register learned that his older brother Sam had died in a New Jersey hospital after complications from open-heart surgery, which had been performed three months earlier. John spent the day sleeping and that afternoon began *See Through* (p. 173), a painting of his son David's hand holding a martini glass in front of a television set whose screen has gone blank.[1]

Register and his family flew to New Jersey, and his sons served as pallbearers. "I couldn't help but look at the funeral as a prequel to my own," Register wrote. "I know in New Orleans they dance happily through the streets after the funeral. I've felt the same exhilaration myself after a funeral. A sort of giddy leap of joy that you aren't the dead one, but not this time. Cathy said, as we were flying home, 'I can't wait to get back to our quiet lives of denial.'"[2]

On May 31 Register went into UCLA hospital with fever, chest pains, nausea and disorientation. A week later he was released with a morphine patch to combat pain in his back, lungs and ribs. The month of June brought weekly emergency visits. The doctors were discouraged by the growth of the tumors, one now the size of a baseball. Cathy was desolate, but John told her, "Bullshit. I'll make it." They gave him three transfusions and he returned home with an oxygen unit.[3]

For the next few months he was in and out of the hospital with tumor fevers. In August, however, a deep bout of depression brought him to a nadir. He fixated on a line from Joseph Conrad's *The Secret Sharer*: "Let them think what they liked, but I didn't mean to drown myself. I meant to swim till I sank — but that's not the same thing." He quoted it when he wrote to Eugene Beck, confessing, "I have been clinically depressed by the true medical definition: Suicidal, sleepless, complete lack of interest in everything, a revulsion in all man's activities.... I've stopped

Self-portrait, 1995
oil on canvas, 16 x 20 inches
Collection of Catherine Register

Opposite:
Man on Road, 1995
oil on canvas, 49 x 70 inches
Collection of Joan Preston O'Neil

Top: *Studio Still Life*, 1995
oil on canvas, 22 x 28 inches
Collection of Martin Muller

Above: *Still Life with Lemons*, 1995
oil on paper, 16 x 20 inches
Collection of Catherine Register

Opposite:
See Through, 1995
oil on canvas, 50 x 35 inches
Collection of Janine Smith

painting these last two months. The process curiously defines my self-worth. I look at the body of work I've produced and feel I've wasted my life. I can't even contemplate starting a painting, not even a simple still life."[4]

Somehow he bounced back. On Cathy's birthday, August 11, he gave her a self-portrait he had just completed (p. 171), based on a 1992 photograph. A week later he started a painting of himself walking down the road in a desert. In a letter he called it *Going Towards the Vanishing Point*, but later changed the title to *Man on Road*, 1995 (p. 170).[5] The man is carrying a suitcase and his hat seems nearly burned away by the sun, much as Register's scalp had been carved away by surgery. Working hard, he finished it in two weeks. He took time out to send 200 invitations to various friends and artists for the upcoming show at Modernism.

John wanted one last major painting for the show and from September 4 through 10 he tapped into a reserve of energy. He wrote Eugene Beck: "I started a painting six days ago. Some paintings take months of tinkering. This one seemed to fall together effortlessly." It was a picture of a bespectacled man seated on the edge of a bed.[6] One Sunday John played chess with a friend, a match so exhausting he slept until 3 the next afternoon; but when he got up he finished the painting *Man on Bed* (p.177). This masterpiece is of an older man. Compactly built, the man bears a strong resemblance to John Fante, with whom Register identified. Yet Cathy remembered that her husband himself often sat like this when he awakened in the morning. "He would perch on the edge of his bed for up to five minutes, collecting his thoughts for the rest of the day." The man in the painting, however, seems to be gathering the recollections of a lifetime and, in facing left, looks back at life rather than to the future.

Three days later, Cathy and John loaded this picture into their Land Cruiser and drove north to San Francisco. The hot drive through the desert and the frenetic rush hour traffic of the city by the Bay left Register anxious and drained. They checked in at the Sheraton Palace Hotel next door to the gallery, and he fell asleep with exhaustion.

At 5 the next evening, the Register family gathered at the hotel. John's daughter Kate took his arm and led him down Market Street to the gallery. His oxygen tank was already waiting in Martin Muller's office. As the collectors and artists

Westward Beach, 1995
oil on canvas, 35 x 50 inches
Collection of Bob and Diane Pryt

arrived, the social blur of handshaking and trying to remember names began. The show was a success, and most of the pictures sold. Register felt weak and was shy about his dramatically scarred face and head. Finding a haven in Muller's private office, he sat in a chair and received friends, admirers, and fellow artists in small groups. Instead of the ordeal of a dinner party with collectors, the Register family retired to the hotel and ordered champagne and room service. The artist wrote a friend: "It was the best after show dinner I've ever had. I sat in a big chair with an ottoman for my shoe-less feet, and had a club sandwich."7

Back in Malibu, on September 24, Cathy awakened in the night to hear John crying from the pain that riddled his chest. Yet the next day, he mustered the strength to start a last masterpiece, *The Light In The Mirror*, completed in 1996 (p. 182). Painted in shades of brown and purple, this picture depicts the same rented room that appeared in *Man on Bed*. There are direct references to the suite of etchings Register created to illustrate Fante's *Ask The Dust*. Only this time, the bed is neatly made, the man is gone, and all that remains is the dim reflection of light in the mirror. It is one of the few interiors Register painted without a visible window or light source.

In early October he had another relapse with high fever. It was caused by bacteria in the Groshank, a permanent valve implanted in his chest to give the physicians easy access to his blood and fluids. He wrote his mother on October 18: "Every painting now feels like a last gasp. I keep telling myself 'one more painting.' There is a part of me that would like to collapse and forget about it, but then at 3:30 in the afternoon the vestige of a work ethic kicks in, and I get to it."8

A week later his old friend from advertising days, Eugene Beck, flew in from Canada so that Register could begin a portrait of him smoking a cigar (above right). In her diary Cathy wrote that John had "a wonderful time" art-directing as son Peter photographed Eugene for the portrait. Cathy noted: "In the evening we had a festive dinner and all tried a little slug of liquid morphine...not a high anyone would want — deadening — but the talk was the best. John very happy to be bullshitting with Eugene."9

Register spent Halloween carving pumpkins with daughter Kate and daughter-in-law Karen. He took great enjoyment in the play of his grandson John Sherman Register II. Three days later he responded to a letter from Hunt Barclay,

Eugene, 1995
oil on canvas, 18 x 18 inches
Collection of Eugene and Kathleen Beck

Register and Martin Muller, 1995. Photograph by Peter Register.

who had praised John for his courage and intelligence: "With false modesty I could give you my definition of courage. It's going into a burning house to save someone. There is an element of choice. I have no choice. I am only enduring what I can't influence. So far I'm only mildly uncomfortable. The prospect of slow strangulation does fill me with terror."[10]

In mid-November John started a painting of a cafe interior, *The Open Door* (p. 181). Cathy's diary noted: "So happy to be painting again. Needs more oxygen to keep painting."[11] An appointment with the oncologist revealed that one lung had shut down entirely. Register finished the portrait of Eugene smoking a cigar at Thanksgiving. That day he wrote his mother: "One of my lungs no longer functions. I have a machine that makes oxygen when you plug it in. I'm tethered to a twenty-foot tube. It irritated my nostrils at first but now, except for the noise, I'm used to it. Cathy lays out my brushes, arranges my palette, on large canvases paints the backgrounds, and cleans the brushes in the evening. I couldn't paint, or live for that matter, without her. I only do about two hours a day, but I've become an amazingly efficient painter."[12]

On Christmas Eve 1995 Cathy noted: "John very sad in the night. The morning was perfect with the family all together and lots of love." John and Cathy were deeply bonded to their children. Eldest son Peter (married to Karen Shumaker) was now a professional photographer, Kate was an artist and teacher, and David was a successful advertising copywriter. There was new excitement in the family as David had become engaged to Victoria Foran.

In January, 1996, John wrote to Martin Muller that he was reading Jane Austen's *Emma* and playing chess with son Peter, but that it was difficult making art, let alone brushing his teeth. "My attempts at works on paper have gone poorly. I think when one's abilities decline it shows up first in the drawing. It came as a great surprise to me because I was able to bring to a reasonable conclusion the painting I had been working on. This comes as a great disappointment to me as I had hoped to be able to do eight or ten good works for the March/April show. Now I wonder if the show is even advisable."[13]

John, Cathy and the children celebrated his 57th birthday at the Malibu house on February 1. The next day he wrote Muller about the painting *Man on Bed*,

Sketch for Prologue to 'Ask the Dust,' 1990
ink and gouache on paper,
14 x 11 inches
Collection of Eileen Battat

Opposite:
Man on Bed, 1995
oil on canvas, 50 x 50 inches
Collection of Paul and
Cindy Levy

saying that there would be no more big pictures like this one: "It saddens me in a way because I think my work was moving in a new direction and that painting is representative of where I wanted my painting to go." He also expressed his gratitude for their business relationship. "You have let me live the life I always wanted for myself. What a force you have been."[14]

Three days later Martin Muller and I flew down to Malibu to discuss the works-on-paper show, to plan the retrospective exhibition at the San Jose Museum of Art and to discuss this book. John seemed in better shape than one would have expected, and Cathy noted that our visit and "enthusiastic response was wonderful for John. He felt he was still part of this world."[15] But the meeting exhausted him and he slept for 14 hours.

In early February Register began coughing up blood. The struggle to live and to be productive was replaced with a decision to die with dignity and comfort. He resigned himself to hospice care at home. He gradually began to say good-bye to his friends through letters. To his close friend George Gage he wrote:

"I read somewhere that the English are a weepy lot once you get past the stiff upper lip. I know it's the case with me....A heart attack in many ways would be easier, but then you don't get the chance to be with the ones you love with crucial knowledge that your time together is finite. Without a question, the person who is dying has it the easiest. I often wake up in the middle of the night and rather than fret about the lost hours of sleep and how it will screw up the painting I wanted to do the next day I can lie there peacefully for hours. I've forgiven myself the sins of my youth, I've forgiven everyone everything....I can't complain."[16]

Register's humor never flagged. To Eugene Beck he wrote: "The hospice lady just left. She was a temp. She came in, sat down, looked deeply in my eyes and said with intimate compassion in her eyes, 'How is the pain?' Thinking about it, it is not a bad introductory line to a complete stranger. I want you to try it at your next few cocktail parties. I think young women might be especially susceptible."[17]

The show comparing drawings by Edward Hopper with Register's works on paper opened at Modernism Gallery on March 2 but John didn't travel north. He wrote his mother, "My show with Edward Hopper is going well. As Hopper is a near deity for me I imagined it would be an affront to link my name with his in an

Cathy, John, Kate, David, Victoria, Peter, Johnny and Karen Register, 1995.

Opposite:
Motel By The Freeway, 1995
oil on canvas, 50 x 70 inches
Collection of Catherine Register

Opposite:
The Open Door, 1996
oil on canvas, 70 x 50 inches
Collection of Catherine Register

Laudromat 1995 (Study for *The Open Door*)
gouache and charcoal,
12 x 8 1/2 inches
Courtesy of Modernism Gallery, San Francisco

exhibition. Martin [Muller] said he did the show so that he could say. 'See, there is the difference, they are very different painters.'"[18]

On April 1, Cathy faxed Eugene Beck: "Things seem to be shutting down. We are scared." John was gasping for air, coughing up blood, and suffering from a septic infection. He requested morphine more and more frequently. Cathy attended to John round the clock. Though he would slip into periods of delirium, he still handwrote letters to be faxed to friends, and when Martin Muller called with gallery business, Cathy recalled that he "snapped into focus" for 20 minutes. Eldest son Peter was around daily, David called from Seattle, and Kate stayed at the house. "She is an amazing comfort to John," wrote Cathy. "Her touch quiets his soul and brings him great happiness and peace. They can jabber away for hours as John fades in and out comfortably.... We are all praying."[19]

John was able to watch a videotape of the Hopper/Register show at Modernism with pleasure, but on April 7 he began to fade. Yet with the morphine there were strange moments of peace and affectionate exchanges with his family. Kate read aloud from a favorite childhood book of his, *The Uncle Wiggly Stories.* In his disorientation he made hand gestures and explained that he was patting his departed dog Lola, who he felt had come back from heaven to visit. He then turned to his daughter and said, "There is someone sitting in a chair over there."

"Who is it?" asked Kate.

Register replied, "Me, as a young man."[20]

In the night and following day he slipped into unconsciousness. Surrounded by his family, on the afternoon of April 9, 1996, John Register died in the arms of his wife.

The funeral service was held at the Registers' house. A hundred family members and friends gathered under the giant coral tree that John had enjoyed gazing at during his last months. His life was celebrated with love, tears and laughter. In one eulogy, Dr. James Forrester said that in all his years in medicine, John was the bravest patient he had ever known.[21]

Illness was not the inspiration for Register's art, but his sense of mortality had tempered and deepened his vision. For Register painting was at once a struggle, an escape and a source of solace. He was rarely satisfied with the results, but each completed painting confirmed his existence. What he achieved in

two decades of painting is memorable and important. Taking into account his illness, it was heroic.

It has been said that an intelligent man thinks of death every day. John Register was one of the smartest men I ever knew well. Always aware of his mortality, he was both tragic and blessed, and he understood this at an early age. He strove to the very end, giving his all, and when youthful exuberance gave way to a stripped-down wisdom, his paintings became an enduring record of 20th-century America.

A few weeks after the funeral, Cathy Register reminisced about her husband in a letter: "Years ago when we would be driving across the country in our Volvo, moving West from New York, John would always stop the car when we hit the lonely desert dotted with sagebrush, make us all get out, and say, 'Be still. Listen to the quiet.' The kids and I would stand motionless by the blazing tarmac. Then he'd pick some sagebrush for us and say, 'That's the best smell in the world. Smell it. That's home! We're West.'"[22]

Opposite:
The Light in the Mirror, 1996
oil on canvas, 47 x 47 Inches
Collection of Catherine Register

Notes

Much of the material that appeared in Barnaby Conrad III's 1989 monograph *John Register* (Chronicle Books) came from taped interviews with the artist and his wife conducted on January 21, 1989. Later, Register corrected and amended the written transcripts. In 1994, the artist contributed handwritten notes for this book.

PREFACE (Pages 14-17)

1. "A realist today must..." Register on realism. Quoted in Mark E. Stegmaier, "John Register," *American Artist*, February 1989, p. 101. With slightly different punctuation (based on Register's handwritten notes) it appeared in Barnaby Conrad III, *John Register* (San Francisco: Chronicle Books, 1989), p. 6.
2. "with Hopper you..." In Conrad, *John Register*, p. 6.

INTRODUCTION (Pages 20-23)

1. "There is no neutral..." E.H. Gombrich, *Art and Illusion* (Princeton, New Jersey: Princeton University Press, 1969), p. 87.
2. "When I drive around LA..." In Conrad, *John Register*, p. 5.
3. "California became..." Shiva Naipaul, *Journey To Nowhere: A New World Tragedy* (New York: Simon and Schuster, 1981).
4. "I feel the pressure of..." John Register to Barnaby Conrad III, letter of March 4, 1989.
5. "They are something..." In Conrad, *John Register*, p. 6.
6. "It's not beautiful furniture..." Ibid., p. 6.

EARLY LIFE (Pages 24-41)

1. "We had anti-aircraft..." In Jeffrey Herr, *John Register: Southern California Paintings*, p. 1. This was the catalog for the exhibition at the Los Angeles Municipal Art Gallery, Barnsdale Art Park, April 20-June 20, 1993.
2. "I was always interested...." In Conrad, *John Register*, p.7.
3. "On the plane..." Register to his mother, Dorothy Pratt Barrett, letter of June 7, 1989.
4. "The biggest influence..." In Conrad, *John Register*, p. 7.
5. "It is not a background..." Register to Barnaby Conrad III, unpublished letter, April 5, 1996 (written four days before his death).
6. "It was strict...." Unpublished notes to Barnaby Conrad III, circa 1989. *Lord of the Flies* was William Golding's 1954 novel about English schoolboys who revert to savagery on a desert island.
7. "We sat in a circle..." In Stegmaier, "John Register," p. 64-65; Register expanded this quote by handwritten notes in 1989 which appeared in Barnaby Conrad III, "Rendering 'Paradise Gone Amok,'" *Gentleman's Quarterly*, July 1991, Vol. 6, No. 7, p. 149.
8. "We did some painting..." Register on friend Hunt Barclay and early painting. In Conrad, *John Register*, p. 7.
9. "We were fifteen... " and two following paragraphs on adventures in Sacramento Delta, down to "...wake him up." Hunt Barclay to Barnaby Conrad III, unpublished letter circa 1989, part of which appeared in Conrad, *John Register*, p. 9-10.
10. "I didn't take any..." In Conrad, "Rendering 'Paradise Gone Amok,'" p. 149.
11. "I thought his major in..." James Shinn to Conrad, letter of April 25, 1996.
12. Register exposed to Beckett's *Godot* in San Francisco. Tom Bissinger to Conrad, unpublished letter, April 5, 1989.
13. "I thought that was where..." and three more paragraphs on Paris quoted in Conrad, *John Register*, p. 10-11. After publication, Register made slight changes to the quotes in handwritten notes; these appeared in Conrad, "Rendering 'Paradise Gone Amok,'" p. 149.
14. "I was unresponsive..." Register on Bay Area Figurative Expressionist school. In Conrad, *John Register*, p. 11.
15. "I set the record..." Register on race-car driving in California. Unpublished handwritten notes to Conrad, circa 1994.
16. "John and his car..." Two quotes from Thomas Quinn in Conrad, "Rendering 'Paradise Gone Amok,'" p. 149, 169.
17. "I hated working..." Register on the difference between art and illustration. In Conrad, *John Register*, p. 14.
18. "I shot stories..." Register in San Francisco. Ibid.
19. David Ogilvy operated..." Ibid., p. 14-15.
20. "On his better days..." Eugene Beck to Conrad, letter of April 5, 1989.
21. "I was almost speechless..." down to "...reservoir that afternoon." In Conrad, *John Register*, p. 15.
22. "Ray Kinstler..." and Art Students League description down to "...maybe even degenerate." Ibid., p. 15-16.

FIRST PAINTINGS (Pages 42-63)

1. "It took me over..." and quote on photo-realism down to "...shot at it, too." In Conrad, *John Register*, p. 34.
2. "I used to have ..." Ibid., p. 35. Register's son Peter recalled that the dream was inspired by *The Snake Pit*, a film which terrified the artist.
3. "I'd been looking..." Register on *Quality Café*. Ibid., p. 35, 38.

4. "The art history aside…" Register on interior-exterior paintings. Ibid. p. 38.

5. "I ended up at…" Register on exhibiting at the David Stuart Gallery. Ibid.

6. "I had just finished…" Register on Johannes Itten, Bauhaus color master. Ibid.

7. Henry J. Seldis, "Art Walk," *Los Angeles Times*, May 6, 1977.

8. "I didn't just paint…" In Conrad, *John Register*, p. 38.

9. "It just happens…" Ibid, p. 38-39.

10. William Matson Roth, an executive at the Matson Lines shipping company, ran unsuccessfully for governor in 1974. His greatest legacy was preserving Ghirardelli Square in San Francisco.

11. "Rendering from a photograph…" In Conrad, *John Register*, p.39.

12. "The pool was…" Register on *Mojave Pool*. Ibid. p. 39

13. Raymond Chandler, *The Long Goodbye* (New York: Vintage Books, 1992).

14. "I tend to agree with Fairfield Porter…" In Conrad, *John Register*, p. 39.

15. "I was driving along…" Register on *Parking Lot By The Ocean*. Ibid., p. 39, 42.

16. Kenneth Baker, "The Beauty of Light and Color," *San Francisco Chronicle*, March 28, 1988, p. D2.

17. Kenneth Baker, "The Illusion of Light in Empty Spaces," *San Francisco Chronicle*, October 2, 1985.

18. "I love Hopper's work…" In Conrad, *John Register*, p. 6.

19. "There is a psychological…" In Conrad, "Rendering 'Paradise Gone Amok,'" p. 149.

A SENSE OF MORTALITY (Pages 64-83)

1. "In 1957, when I was…" In Conrad, *John Register*, p. 43.

2. "I painted some…" Ibid., p. 46.

3. "They were wristy…" In Stegmaier, "John Register," p. 109.

4. "You have to monitor…" Catherine Register on her husband's health. In Conrad, *John Register*, p. 46.

5. "The picture contains…" Register on *Office*. Ibid., p. 47.

6. "In some ways…" Register on *Two Telephones*, 1985. Register's handwritten notes to Conrad, circa 1989.

7. Michael Gahagan, "John Register: A Painter for Southern California Reasons," *Santa Barbara Magazine*, Summer 1981, p. 72-77.

8. "Parallels to the East Hampton…" Register to John Martin, letter of September 4, 1981.

9. "I feel like I haven't…" Register to John Martin, letter of February 20, 1982.

10. "Made me nostalgic…" Register to John Martin, unpublished letter, March 6, 1982.

Suitcase, 1994
oil on paper, 22 x 15 inches
Courtesy of Modernism Gallery, San Francisco

11. "Fante was a lonely…" In Conrad, *John Register*, p. 65.

12. "I was taking…" On meeting Fante, Halloween, 1975. Ibid. Fante's novel *West of Rome* was published by Black Sparrow Press, 1986.

13. "The last year…" Register to John Martin, letter of July 20, 1982.

14. "As a deeply interested…" John Martin to Register, undated letter circa July 1982.

15. Martin Muller (born 1953) was a French-speaking native of Geneva, Switzerland, who founded Modernism Gallery of San Francisco in 1979.

16. "subtly calling into question…" and "In the early days…" Thomas Albright, "New Perspective in Photo Realism," *San Francisco Chronicle*, October 22, 1982.

17. "I'm back in my studio…" Register to John Martin, letter of November 4, 1982.

18. "I'm finally off the painterly…" Register to John Martin, letter of March 17, 1983.

19. "They put me into a ward…" In Conrad, *John Register*, p. 72.

20. "John is working…" Cathy Register to John Martin, letter of November 17, 1983.

THE RETURN TO THE WEST (Pages 84-119)

1. "Just me, my wife…" In Barnaby Conrad III, "Los Angeles: The New Mecca," *Horizon*, January/February 1987, p. 28.

2. "My son Peter…" and "I had an epidural…" In Conrad, *John Register*, p. 73. Register later amended his original quote with handwritten notes in 1989 for Conrad's profile "Rendering 'Paradise Gone Amok,'" in *GQ* magazine.

3. Kenneth Baker, "The Illusion of Light in Empty Spaces."

4. "It's not so much…" Register on *Desert Restaurant*. In Conrad, *John Register*, p. 76.

5. "I don't mind seeing a few friends…" Ibid., p. 76.

6. "I like the social commentary…" Ibid., p. 76.

7. Lillian Ross, "Talk of the Town," *The New Yorker*, June 9, 1986. p. 29-31.

8. "Driving through the town…" Register on *Mojave Couple*. In Conrad, *John Register*, p. 77.

9. "Across the aisle…" Register on *Man Seated in Restaurant*. Ibid., p. 77.

10. "I was called for jury duty…" Register on *Suits*. Ibid., p. 80.

11. This interpretation of "suits" may have occurred to the collector who bought the painting, Bernie Brillstein, a well-known Los Angeles television producer who eventually purchased five Register paintings.

12. "The three children…" and "I had a bag…" Register on traveling by train. In Conrad, *John Register*, p. 80.

13. "The train offers…" Register to Martin Muller, post card circa June 16, 1988.

14. A French publisher used Register's painting *The Loop* on the cover of the translation of Paul Theroux's 1991 murder novel *Chicago Loop*.

15. "There's something fascinating…" In Conrad, *John Register*, p. 81.

16. "I knew there was something…" and "It's pretty rundown…" Register on *Chicago*. Ibid., p. 84.

17. "I draw a basic outline…" Register's unpublished handwritten notes of 1988, which were partially published in Stegmaier, "John Register," p.102.

18. "That way I can look…" Register on his wife's role as critic. In Conrad, *John Register*, p. 84.

19. "I may start the painting…" Ibid.

20. "For me realism…" Ibid.

21. "Every painting starts…" Register to Conrad, letter of March 4, 1989.

LATE YEARS (Pages 120-169)

1. "I've had a lot of practice…" Register to his mother, letter of August 10, 1989.

2. The silk-screen *Hollywood* was published in an edition of 75 by Wassermann Silkscreen Co. in Santa Monica in 1989.

3. "I found him to be a sweet…" Register on Bukowski. Register to Conrad, letter of November 11, 1994.

4. At Martin Muller's request, Register did a small hand-colored black-and-white lithograph similar to his painting *Train Compartment*, 1990. The edition of 110 signed prints were given as party favors and never sold to the public.

5. "I'm ambivalent about New York…" Register to Conrad, letter of February 18, 1990.

6. The printer who helped Register with the *Ask The Dust* project was the painter Valentin Popov, a recent immigrant from Ukraine. Eric Johnson of Okeanos Press printed 75 copies of the book with hand-set type.

7. The large silk-screen prints *Venetian Light* (image size: 43 x 36 inches) and *Wasteland Hotel* (image size: 33 1/2 x 48 1/2 inches) were printed in editions of 85 at the Wassermann Sillkscreen Co. in Santa Monica in 1990.

8. "Blake did a painting…" Register to Conrad on *The Swimmer* and death, letter of November 11, 1994.

9. "I truly have no idea…" Register to Eugene Beck, letter of June 3, 1992.

10. "I want people to see…" In Gahagan, "John Register: A Painter for Southern California Reasons," p. 74.

11. "existential outlook presents…" Jeffrey Herr, *John Register: Southern California Paintings*, p. 1.

12. "I am struggling with…" Register to his mother, letter of April 1, 1994. The description of Bukowski's face was inspired by Bukowski's obituary in the *Los Angeles Times*, which mentioned a previous *Los Angeles Times Magazine* article written in 1987 by Paul Ciotti, who described Bukowski's nose as looking as if it was "assembled from Studebaker hoods and Buick fenders."

13. "Halfway through the shoot…" Register to Conrad on photograph session for *The Martini*, unpublished handwritten notes, 1994.

14. "When I was young…" In Barnaby Conrad III, *The Martini* (San Francisco: Chronicle Books, 1995), p. 97.

15. "There was a large new painting…" Register to his mother on *Vacancy*, letter of October 28, 1994.

16. "It was so final.…" Register to his mother, letter of November 4, 1994.

17. "existential Christian…" Register to his mother, letter of December 12, 1994.

18. "Your blessing was…" Register to The Most Reverend Robert S. Morse, letter of December 16, 1994.

19. "I think I will do it…" Register to George and Beth Gage, unpublished letter of February 24, 1995.

20. Register also attempted a larger (50 x 70 inches) version of *Drowning in Hollywood* in which the young man in a suit lies in a coffin-like bathtub.

GOING TOWARDS THE VANISHING POINT (Pages 170-183)

1. Register starts *See Through*. Catherine Register diary entry, May 8, 1995.

2. "I couldn't help but look…" Register to Hunt Barclay, letter of May 15, 1995.

3. Register's hospital visits. Catherine Register diary entries of May 31-June 25, 1995.

4. Joseph Conrad quote, "Let them think…" and Register's, "I have been clinically…" Register to Eugene Beck, undated letter circa June 1995.

5. Change of title on *Man on Road*. Cathy Register, diary entry, August 18, 1995.

6. "I started a painting..." Register to Eugene Beck, letter of September 13, 1995.

7. "It was the best after show dinner..." Register to Eugene Beck, letter of September 22, 1995.

8. "Every painting now feels..." Register to his mother, letter of October 18, 1995.

9. "In the evening..." Catherine Register, diary entry of October 21, 1995.

10. "With false modesty ..." Register to Hunt Barclay, letter of November 2, 1995.

11. "So happy to be..." Catherine Register, diary entry of November 17, 1995.

12. "One of my lungs..." Register to his mother, letter of November 27, 1995.

13. "My attempts at works on paper..." Register to Martin Muller, undated letter circa January 1996.

14. "It saddens me..." Register to Martin Muller, letter of February 2, 1996.

15. "enthusiastic response..." Catherine Register, diary entry of February 5, 1996.

16. "I read somewhere..." Register to George Gage, letter of February 14, 1996.

17. "The hospice lady..." Register to Eugene Beck, undated letter circa February 1996.

18. "My show with Hopper..." Register to his mother, letter of March 16, 1996.

19. "She is an amazing comfort..." Catherine Register to Eugene Beck, letter of April 7, 1996.

20. Register's last moments and "There is someone sitting..." Catherine Register, diary entry of April 7, 1996.

21. Bishop Robert Morse led the service. Nearly everyone mentioned in this book was there, including Register's wheelchair-bound 88-year-old mother.

22. "Years ago when we..." Catherine Register to Eugene Beck, undated letter circa May 1996.

JOHN REGISTER
Selected Bibliography

Albright, Thomas. "New Perspectives in Photo Realism." *San Francisco Chronicle*, Oct. 22, 1982, p. 71.

Andrews, Colman. "Art of the State/California." *New West Magazine*, Jan. 1981, pp. 56.

Baker, Kenneth. "The Face of a Mood." *Connoisseur*, Dec. 1990, p. 44.

—, "The Illusion of Light in Empty Spaces." *San Francisco Chronicle*, Oct. 2, 1985, p. 59.

—, "Vision of the West: The Beauty of Light and Color," *San Francisco Chronicle*, March 28, 1988, D2.

Ballatore, Sandy. "Editing Reality," *Artweek*. Vol. 6. No. 35, Oct. 18, 1975, p. 3-4.

Bonetti, David. "The Seat of His Alienation," *San Francisco Examiner*, Oct. 16, 1991, p. D3.

Browning, Jeffrey. *John Register*, Black Sparrow Press/Modernism, Santa Barbara/San Francisco, 1985.

Clark, Tom. "Art That Brightens an Ordinary World" (review of Barnaby Conrad III, *John Register*), *San Francisco Chronicle*, Jan. 25, 1990, p. E5.

Conrad III, Barnaby. *John Register*, Chronicle Books. San Francisco, 1989.

—, "Los Angeles: The New Mecca," *Horizon*, Vol. 30, No. 1, Jan./Feb. 1987, p. 17-20.

—, "Rendering 'Paradise Gone Amok'," *Gentlemen's Quarterly*, July 1991, p. 148-149 & 169-170.

Davis, Randal. "Fixed on Facts," *Artweek*, Vol. 24, No. 23, Dec. 2 1993, p. 23.

Ewing, Robert. *Contemporary California Artists 33: John Register* (exhibition catalogue), Laguna Art Museum, Laguna Beach, 1986.

Frankenstein, Alfred. "A View from Santa Monica," *San Francisco Chronicle*, May 11, 1978.

Gahagan, Michael. "John Register, Southern California Painter," *Santa Barbara Magazine*, Vol. 7, No. 2, Summer, 1981, p. 72-77.

Harrison, Helen A. "49 Artists Capture the Illusions and Realities of Winter," *New York Times*, Jan. 3, 1982.

—, "Lively Experiments with the Still Life," *New York Times*, May 3, 1981.

Herr, Jeffrey. "*John Register: Southern California Paintings*" (exhibition catalogue), L.A. Municipal Art Gallery, Barnsdall Art Park, Los Angeles, 1993.

Los Angeles Times, May 30, 1993

Muchnic, Suzanne. "Mind-Etching Visions by Register, Richards," *Los Angeles Times*, July 18, 1986, Part VI, p. 14.

Nolte, Carl. "John Register" (obituary), *San Francisco Chronicle*, April 11, 1996.

Oliver, Myrna. "John Sherman Register; Painter of L.A. Cityscapes," (obituary) *Los Angeles Times*, April 13, 1996.

Pinchbeck, Daniel. "Openings," *Art & Antiques*, Vol. XV. No. 6, summer 1993, p. 28.

Rohrer, Judith. "John Register's Luminous Interiors," *Artweek*, May 20, 1978, p. 5.

Ross, Lillian. "Talk of the Town," *The New Yorker*, June 9, 1986, p. 29-31.

Seldis, Henry J. "Art Walk," *Los Angeles Times*, May 6, 1977.

Stegmaier, Mark E. "John Register," *American Artist*, Vol. 53, Issue 559, Feb. 1989, p. 64-67 & 99-102.

Wilson, William. "Distinction in Realist Paintings," *Los Angeles Times*, June 17, 1982.

Wortz, Melinda. *Pasadena Collects: An Overview* (exhibition catalogue), Pasadena Art Alliance, 1986.

JOHN REGISTER
Chronology

Born New York City, 1939; died Malibu, Calif., 1996

EDUCATION

University of California, Berkeley, B.A., Literature, 1961

California School of Fine Arts, San Francisco, 1959-60

Art Center School of Design, Los Angeles, 1962-63

Pratt Institute, studies in design and television, 1964

ONE-PERSON EXHIBITIONS

1999 "John Register: A Retrospective," San Jose Museum of Art, San Jose

1995 Modernism, San Francisco

1993 Modernism, San Francisco

Los Angeles Municipal Art Gallery, Los Angeles

Earl McGrath Gallery, Los Angeles

1992 Kirby Art Center Gallery, Lawrenceville School, Lawrenceville, N.J.

1991 Modernism, San Francisco

1990 "Works on Paper," Modernism, San Francisco

1988 Modernism/Art L.A. 88, Los Angeles

Pepperdine University, Malibu

1986 "California Contemporary Artists 33; John Register," Laguna Art Museum, Laguna Beach

1985 Modernism, San Francisco

1982 Modernism, San Francisco

1981 Malibu Art & Design, Malibu

1980 Elaine Benson Gallery, Bridgehampton, N.Y.

1979 Boehm Gallery, San Diego

1978 William Sawyer Gallery, San Francisco

1977 David Stuart Gallery, Los Angeles

1975 David Stuart Gallery, Los Angeles

SELECTED GROUP EXHIBITIONS

1996 "Edward Hopper/John Register: Works on Paper," Modernism, San Francisco

1995 "The Collector's Eye; Works from Alumni Collections," Kirby Art Center Gallery, Lawrenceville School, Lawrenceville, N.J.

1994 "Wheels," Track 16, Bergamot Station, Santa Monica

"46th Annual American Academy Purchase Exhibition," American Academy of Arts and Letters, New York City

1993 "Interiors" Tortue Gallery, Santa Monica

1992 Richard York Gallery, New York City

1991 "The Palm Tree Show; New Paintings by Eleven Artists," Modernism, San Francisco

1990 "Collector's Choice; Prints for the '90s," Santa Monica Heritage Museum, Santa Monica

1986 "Francis J. Greenburger Foundation Award Exhibition," Ruth Siegel Gallery, New York City

Laguna Art Museum, Laguna Beach

"Pasadena Collects the Art of Our Time," Pasadena Art Alliance in cooperation with Pasadena Art Center College of Design

1983 "California Drawings," Modernism, San Francisco

"Selections from the Permanent Collection," Guild Hall Museum, East Hampton, N.Y.

"The Parrish Invitational '83," The Parrish Museum, Southampton, N.Y.

"The Long Island Landscape," The Water Mill Museum, Water Mill, N.Y.

"City," French Gallery, New York City

1982 Bologna & Landi Gallery, East Hampton, N.Y.

"Southern California Realist Painting," Laguna Art Museum, Laguna Beach

"Photorealism Revisited," Molly Barnes Gallery, Los Angeles

"Winterscape," Guild Hall Museum, East Hampton, N.Y.

1981 "Still Life Paintings and Drawings by East End Artists," The Parrish Museum, Southampton, N.Y.

"The Artist in the Park," Hirschl & Adler Galleries, New York City

1978 "New Talent," Thomas Segal Gallery, Boston

"Realist Painters, Los Angeles," ARCO Center for Visual Art, Los Angeles

1977 "Cityscapes," The Fine Arts Museums of San Francisco

SELECTED AWARDS

1986 The Francis J. Greenburger Foundation Award

SELECTED PUBLIC COLLECTIONS

Arkansas Arts Center, Little Rock, Ark.

Deutsches Postmuseum, Frankfurt, Germany

Fine Arts Museums of San Francisco, San Francisco

Guild Hall Museum, East Hampton, N.Y.

Kirby Art Center, Lawrenceville School, Lawrenceville, N.J.

Laguna Art Museum, Laguna Beach

Parrish Museum, Southampton, N.Y.

San Francisco Museum of Modern Art, San Francisco

San Jose Museum of Art Board of Trustees

Officers

George H. Cole, Jr., President
Mary Davidge, Vice President
Terry McCarthy, Treasurer
Barbara Shapiro, Secretary

Trustees

Gregory K. Belanger
Sue Bisceglia
Sandra L. Churchill
James R. Compton
Mary C. Covello
William Faulkner
Toby Fernald
Margie Fernandes, Vice Mayor
Drew Gibson
Jane V. Goldbach
Hon. Nazario Gonzales
Kit Hinrichs
Ryan Nguyen Hubris
Katharine Imwalle
Mark E. Jensen
Martha J. Kanter
Robert H. Kustel
Van Thi Le
Michael J. Levinthal
Kathryn Lewis
Peter W. Lipman
Magda Madriz
T. Michael Nevens
Barbara D. Oshman
David J. Perez
Gerald H. Polk
Deborah Rappaport
Mark H. Ritchie
John E. Rossell, III
Harry J. Saal
Tina M. Sankoff-Dixon
Dick Watts

Staff of the San Jose Museum of Art

Pilar Agüero	Associate Director of Education, Museum School	Cheryl Kiddoo	Education Partners Coordinator
Lucille Alemania	Bookkeeping Assistant	Karen Kienzle	Curatorial Assistant
Susan Armas	Administrative Assistant to the Director	Cathy Kimball	Acting Senior Curator
Leslie Barton	Manager of Retail Operations	Wendy Kirst	Director of Special Gifts
Kaela Bernal	Assistant to the Deputy Director	Christine Landrum	Membership Director
Judy Blankenburg	Development Associate	Diane Maxwell	Director of Communications
Lorran Bronnar	Corporate Events Manager	Margaret Maynard	Curator of Education, Interpretation
Stacy Brown	Communications Assistant	Angela McConnell	Director of Development
Hannah Cahalan	Bookkeeper	Stephanie Mitzenmacher	Membership Coordinator
Josi Callan	Director	Thea Namundjebo	Receptionist and Admissions Supervisor
Judi Casanova	Museum Store Sales Associate and Volunteer Coordinator	Yvonne Nevens	Director of Marketing
		Deborah Norberg	Deputy Director
Valerie DeLang	Museum Educator for School and Teacher Programs	Randall Packer	Multimedia Director
		Stephanie Parkhurst	Registrar
Annette Eldredge	Manager of Special Events and Museum Tours	John Renzel	Facilities Manager
Betty Jo Ewing	Events Assistant	Marlyn Rivero	Administrative Assistant, Director's Office
Bill Farr	Manager of Corporate and Foundation Gifts	Grace Y. Salk	Education Coordinator for Museum School Services and Kids ArtSundays
Kathryn Fernandes	Art School Assistant		
Steven Haigh	Manager of Computer Services	Lynne Schuyler-King	Business Manager
Patricia Hickson	Assistant Curator	Dean Silvestri	Museum Store Assistant Manager
Roger Jens	Museum Store Sales Associate	Ellie Smith	Admissions Supervisor
Richard Karson	Chief of Design and Installation	Vern Trindade	Assistant Preparator

Exhibition Checklist

Paintings

All dimensions are in inches; height precedes width.

Self-portrait, 1971
 oil on cardboard, 16 x 12

Hotel with Four Chairs, 1974
 oil on canvas, 45 x 45

Philippe's Sandwich Shop, 1974
 oil on canvas, 30 x 44

Drive-through Donut Shop, 1975
 oil on canvas, 31 x 49

Mustang Cafe, 1975
 oil on canvas, 33 x 43

Green Chair, 1976
 oil on canvas, 40 x 40

Parking Lot by the Ocean, 1976
 oil on canvas, 31 x 48

Motel, 1977
 oil on canvas, 50 x 50

Venetian Light, 1977
 oil on canvas, 42 x 49 1/4

Mojave Bus Station, 1978
 oil on canvas, 28 1/2 x 39 1/2

Oxnard Pizza, 1978
 oil on canvas, 45 x 45

Office, 1982
 oil on canvas, 40 x 50

Waiting Room, 1982
 oil on canvas, 50 x 61

Yellow Couch, 1982
 oil on canvas, 45 x 45

Coney Island BMT, 1983
 oil on canvas, 48 3/4 x 48 3/4

Laundromat, 1983
 oil on canvas, 50 x 50

Waiting Room for the Beyond, 1983
 oil on canvas, 50 x 55

Bus Station, 1984
 oil on canvas, 50 x 70

Cadillac Hotel, 1984
 oil on canvas, 50 x 70

Cafe Winter, 1984
 oil on canvas, 50 x 50

Southwest Motel, 1984
 oil on canvas, 50 x 50

Los Angeles, 1985
 oil on canvas, 50 x 70

Office Chairs, 1985
 oil on canvas, 50 x 70

Te Amo, 1985
 oil on canvas, 50 x 91

Desert Restaurant, 1986
 oil on canvas, 50 x 70

Man Seated in Restaurant, 1987
 oil on canvas, 50 x 50

Mojave Couple, 1987
 oil on canvas, 40 x 90

Purple Chair, 1987
 oil on canvas, 70 x 50

Study for 'Waiting Room for the Beyond,'
 1987, oil on canvas, 24 x 24

Backyard, 1988
 oil on canvas, 35 x 50

The Counter, 1988
 oil on canvas, 50 x 50

Watching the Storm (Denver), 1988
 oil on canvas, 40 x 90

Bunker Hill, 1989
 oil on canvas, 35 x 50

Lost Bus, 1989
 oil on canvas, 49 x 72

Pacific Rim Restaurant, 1989
 oil on canvas, 50 x 70

Texas Cafe, 1989
 oil on canvas, 50 x 70

Wasteland Hotel, 1989
 oil on canvas, 49 x 70

Waiting at the Terminal (Airport), 1990-91
 oil on canvas, 70 x 49

Houses Near Freeway, 1991
 oil on canvas, 35 x 50

Mesa Cafe, 1991
 oil on canvas, 50 x 70

Frankie & Johnny, 1992
 oil on canvas, 35 x 50

Gallup Still Life, 1993
 oil on canvas, 35 x 50

Hotel by Railroad, 1993
 oil on canvas, 35 x 50

Three Tables, 1993
 oil on canvas, 50 x 50

Times Square, 1993
 oil on canvas, 50 x 90

Two Red Stools, 1993
 oil on canvas, 35 x 50

Desert Gas Station, 1994
 oil on canvas, 40 x 50

Martini, 1994
 oil on canvas, 50 x 35

Twin Arrows Cafe, 1994
 oil on canvas, 22 x 28

Vacancy, 1994
 oil on canvas, 40 x 50

Late Afternoon Light, 1994-1995
 oil on canvas, 40 x 50

The Colorado, 1995
 oil on canvas, 50 x 70

Man on Bed, 1995
 oil on canvas, 50 x 50

Man on Road, 1995
 oil on canvas, 49 x 70

Motel by the Freeway, 1995
 oil on canvas, 50 x 70

See Through, 1995
 oil on canvas, 50 x 35

Self-portrait, 1995
 oil on canvas, 16 x 20

The Light in the Mirror, 1996
 oil on canvas, 47 x 47

Open Door, 1996
 oil on canvas, 50 x 40

Works on Paper

Laguna Canyon, 1973
 oil on paper, 20 x 16

Study for 'Parking Lot by the Ocean,' 1976
 pencil on paper, 12 x 17-1/2

Study for 'Restaurant by the Sea,' 1985
 ink and colored pencil on paper

Red Booths, 1986
 silk-screen, edition: 85
 28 x 43

Study for 'Desert Restaurant,' 1986
 oil on paper, 16 x 20

Waiting Room for the Beyond, 1988
 silk-screen, edition: 85, 35 x 35

Hollywood, 1989
 silk-screen, edition: 75
 14 3/4 x 11 1/4

Cadillac Hotel, 1990
 etching, edition: 30, 15-1/2 x 22

Martin Muller, 1990
 etching, edition: 19, 6 x 6

Oak Chair, 1990
 etching, edition: 30, 8 x 8

Prologue for 'Ask the Dust,' 1990
 seven etchings, edition: 125, 5 x 5

Restaurant, 1990
 etching, edition: 19, 6 x 6

Train Station, 1990
 etching, edition: 24, 6 x 6

Venetian Light, 1990
 multimedia print, edition: 85
 36 x 43

Waiting Room, 1990
 etching, edition: 40, 8 x 8

Wasteland Hotel, 1990
 silk-screen, edition: 85,
 33 1/2 x 48 1/2

Suitcase, 1994
 oil on paper, 26 1/2 x 20

Lenders to the Exhibition

Molly Barnes and Joe Mock
John and Susan Caldwell
Frederick and Nina Carroll
Mr. and Mrs. Duncan A. Chapman
Barnaby Conrad III
Winston Stuart Conrad
Chuck and Becky Daggs
Karen and John Diefenbach
Rick and Dana Dirickson
Mandy and Cliff Einstein
Mr. and Mrs. Michael S. Engl
Larry and Joan Evans
Morgan Flagg and Elizabeth Ross Flagg
George and Beth Gage
Art Kern
Suzanne and Guy Lampard
Paul and Cindy Levy
Mr. and Mrs. W. Huston Lillard III
John and Barbara Martin/
 Black Sparrow Press
J. Michael and Marjorie A. Matthews
Barbara and Richard Mendelsohn
Modernism Gallery
Martin Muller
Penny and Noel Nellis
Joan Preston O'Neil
Tom Patchett
Bob and Diane Pryt
Catherine Register
David and Victoria Register
Kathryn Register
Leslie Register
Peter and Karen Register
Janine Smith
Garen and Sharalyn King Staglin
Peter E. Thieriot
Jeffrey and Evelyne Thomas
Margret Jhin and Peter A. Walsh
Mr. and Mrs. Anthony Weir
Several Private Collectors

Index

Académie Julian, 31
Actor's Workshop, San Francisco, 31
Albers, Josef, 32
Albright, Thomas, 81
Anderson, Lennart, 41
Art in America, 43
Art Students League (NY), 41, 43
Austen, Jane, *Emma*, 176
Backyard, 113
Baker, Kenneth, 62, 93-94
Bakersfield, 121, 122
Banham, Rayner, 16
Barclay, Hunt, 28-30, 175
Barrett, Dorothy Pratt, 25-26, 161, 162, 175, 176, 180
Barrett, Stephen, 26
Barrett, William, 25, 26,
Beach Boys, The, 67
Beck, Eugene, 40, 137, 171, 172, 175, 176, 180
Beckett, Samuel, *Waiting for Godot*, 31
Bibliography, 188
Big Brother, 56, 56, 165
Bischoff, Elmer, 32
Bissinger, Tom, 30-31
Black Sparrow Press, 70, 75, 93
Blue Chair, 83, 83
Boehm Gallery, 62
Bresson, Henri-Cartier, 97
Brooklyn, 75
Brooklyn Chess Club, 36
Brooks, James, 62,
Brooks School, 26
Browning, Jeffrey, 93
Bukowski, 161
Bukowski, Charles, 70, 75, 81, 105, 121, 121, 161
   Hollywood, 105
Bunker Hill, 2-3, 121
Burchfield, Charles, 97
Burrito, 158
Bus Station, 85, 86
Cadillac Grill with Flags, 42, 43
Cadillac Hotel, 17, 132
Cafe Winter, 85, 87
California School of Fine Arts, 32
Callan, Josi, 13
Chandler, Raymond, 57
   The Long Goodbye, 56
Chicago, 115, 117
Chronology, 189
Closed Restaurant, 48, 49, 56
Club Delta, 29, 29
Colorado, 160, 161

Conrad, Barnaby III, 85, 115, 119, 179
Conrad, Joseph, 75
   The Secret Sharer, 171
Conversation, 142
Cottingham, Richard, 43
Counter, The, 114, 115
Crawford, Ralston, 16, 43
Crumb, Robert, 81
cummings, e.e., 31
Curtain in the Wind, 82
Curtains in the Wind, 143
Danovitch, Dr. Gabriel, 168
Dash, Robert, 62, 67
David Stuart Gallery, 50
De Chirico, 17
de Kooning, Willem, 62
de Hooch, Pieter, 48
Desert Diner, 121, 125
   Study for, 15
Desert Gas Station, 167
Desert Restaurant, 94, 95
   Study for, 94
Diebenkorn, Richard, 97
Diehl, Guy, 161
Diner With Red Seats, 99
Dining Car, 78, 80
Drive-through Donut Shop, 50, 51
Drowning in Hollywood, 165, 168
Dunaway, Faye, 105
Earl McGrath Gallery, 158
Earth magazine, 38
Eastman, Chuck, 33
Eckart, Charles, 34
Elektra Films, 36
Emmerich, André, 97
Estes, Richard, 15, 43, 50
Eugene, 175, 175
Faded Flag, 43, 43
Fante, John, 52, 70, 75-76, 76, 132, 172
   Ask the Dust, 76, 132, 175
   Dreams From Bunker Hill, 75
   West of Rome, 76
Fast Food, 112
Fine Arts Museums of San Francisco, 62
Fischl, Eric, 97, 105
Foran, Victoria, 176
Forrester, Dr. James, 89, 183
Four Phone Booths, 45, 68
Four Telephone Booths, 44
Francis J. Greenburger Foundation, 97
Frank, Robert, 38
Frankie & Johnny, 144
Franklin, Dr. Stan, 85
Fresno, 146-147
Friedlander, Lee, 38
Gage, George and Beth, 165, 179
Gallup Still Life, 153

Gas, Food, 5
Gerard Drive, 81
Girl on the Chaise, 41, 165
Glaspy, Dr. John, 168
Goings, Ralph, 15, 43
Gombrich, E. H., 21
Green Chair, 13
Greenburg, Clement, 97
Helnwein, Gottfried, 81, 161
Herr, Jeffrey, 158
Hockney, David, 56
Hollywood, 121
Hollywood Hornet, 52
Hopper, Edward, 15-16, 62, 81, 48, 180
Hotel d'Alsace, 31
Hotel by Railroad, 154
Hotel in Desert, 127
Hotel with Four Chairs, 46, 47
Houses Near Freeway, 140
Howell, Wendy, 29
Interchange, 14
Interrogation, 129
Interstate Cafe, 102, 121
Itten, Johannes, 52
Jamaica Avenue, 66
John Register, 1988 monograph, 52, 115, 121
Johns, Jasper, 43
Jones, James, 32
Journey, 149
Kelly, Ellsworth, 16
Kierkegaard, Søren, 17
King, Rodney, 137
Kinstler, Everett Raymond, 41
Krasner, Lee, 62
Kiefer, Anselm, 97
L.A. at Dawn, 150-151
L.A. Riots, 158, 159
La Brea Motel, 145
Last of the Old City, 110
Late Afternoon Light, 155
Laundromat, 63
Lawrenceville School, The, 28
Leaving L.A. on the Desert Wind, 126
Lewis, Wyndham, 70
   The Apes of God, 75
Light in the Mirror, 175, 182
Lobby, 97
Long Island Expressway, 78
Long Island Expressway Tollgate, 93
Loop, 115, 116
Los Angeles, 93, 93-94
Los Angeles Municipal Art Gallery, 158
Los Angeles Times, 52
Lost Bus, 111
Lunch, 157
Magnolia Editions, 132
Malevich, Kasemir, 81

Malibu Art & Design, 67
Man in Reflected Light, 148
Man on Bed, 15, 172, 175, 176, 177
Man on the Road (Going Towards the Vanishing Point), 170, 172
Man Seated in a Restaurant, 104, 105
   Study for, 105
Manchurian Candidate, The, 40
Manet, Edouard, *Dejeuner sur l'herbe*, 105
Manhattan Walking Bridge, 16, 16, 58
Marca-Relli, Conrad, 62
Martin, John, 75, 76, 81, 83, 121
Martini, The (book), 161
Martini, 161, 164
Mason, Frank, 28
Maugham, Somerset, 32
McCaffrey & McCall, 36
McCann-Erickson, 34
McCoy, Ann, 28
McCoy, Deny, 28
McLaughlin, John, 16
McQueen, Steve, 34
Mencken, H. L., 75
Mesa Cafe, 137
Messer, Tom, 97
Midtown, 85, 93
Modernism Gallery, 78, 93, 165, 172, 180
Mojave Bus Station, 68, 71
Mojave Couple, 105, 106-107
Mojave Desert, 98
Mojave Pool, 17, 56, 162
Motel, 56
Motel by the Freeway, 168, 178
Motel: Route 66, 131
Morse, Bishop Robert S., 165
Motherwell, Robert, 97
Muller, Martin, 78, 81, 121, 122, 137, 165, 172, 175, 175, 176, 179, 180
Mustang Cafe 47, 48, 50
Mustard Jar, 100
Naipul, Shiva, 22
Nebraska, 102-103
New York Commerical Chess League, 36
New Yorker, 105
Nitsch, Hermann, 81
Norman, Frank, 'Fings Ain't Wot They Used T' Be,' 32
Notes, 184-187
Oakland, 141
Office, 68, 69, 78
   Study for, 68
Office Chairs, 96
Ogilvy & Mather, 38
Ogilvy, David, 38, 40
Olive Motel, 57
Oliveira, Nathan, 32

Open Door, The, 176, 181
   Study for, 180
Orange Storefront, 65, 65
Orwell, George, 56
Overpass, 16, 44
Overpass Near Rincon, 67, 67
Oxnard Pizza, 52, 54
Pacific Coast Highway, 25
Pacific Rim Restaurant, 23, 119, 132
Parking Lot by the Ocean, 58, 59
   Study for, 58
Philippe's Sandwich Shop, 20
Phone by the Sea, 68
Piaf, Edith, 32
Porter, Fairfield, 67
Portrait of Martin Muller, 115
Pratt, Charles, 36
Pratt Institute, 36
Purple Chair, 85
Quality Cafe, 48, 48
Quinn, Thomas, 26, 34
Ramos, Mel, 161
Red Booths, 52, 55
Register, Barbara, 25, 65, 66
Register, Catherine, 34, 35, 36, 40-41, 43, 50, 65, 68, 83, 89, 105, 108, 119, 158, 165, 168, 171, 172, 175, 179-180, 183
Register, David, 36, 68, 176, 180
Register, John,
   birth of, 25
   childhood of, 25, 26
      as young man, 28-30, 30
   careers in,
      advertising, 34, 36, 38, 39-40
      photography, 38
      criticism of, 62, 81, 93, 162
   death of, 183
      funeral, 183
   education of,
      Art Center (Los Angeles), 34
      Art Students League, 41
      childhood, 26, 28
      Pratt Institute, 34
      University of California at Berkeley, 30, 32
   exhibitions, see 'Chronology,' 188
   family, 179
      children and, 36, 44, 93, 175-176
      death of brother, 171
      father and, 26
      marriage of, 36
      pets of, 165
      wife and, 34, 165
   health of, 22, 65-66, 68, 81, 85, 89, 93, 162, 168, 171, 175, 179-180

   hobbies,
      auto racing, 32, 33, 33-34
      chess, 36, 36
      iceboat racing, 68
      surfing, 43-44, 62, 93
   imagery of,
      cafes and restaurants, 22, 48, 52, 93
      cars, 43
      chairs, 52
      clothing, 108
      deserts, 93
      figures, 105
      streets, 48, 50
      swimming pools, 56
      trains, 115
      telephones, 44, 47, 68, 69
      urban life, 115
   influences on,
      artists, 97
      Barclay, Hunt, 28
      Beckett, Samuel, 31
      Bishoff, Elmer, 32
      Bukowski, Charles, 75
      Chandler, Raymond, 52
      Estes, Richard, 15
      Fante, John, 75-76
      Goings, Ralph, 15
      literature, 72, 75
      Los Angeles, 15, 16, 21,
      mortality, 183
      mother, 26
      Southern California, 58
      West, the, 22
      wife, 119
      Wyeth, Andrew, 28, 28
   paintings
      descriptions of, 15-17, 21-22
      early works, 42-63
      final works, 170-183
      later works, 64-169
      photography and, 56
      struggles with, 78
      techniques of, 116, 119
      use of light and, 16-17
   photographs by, 37, 38, 39, 84
   photographs of, 18-19, 24, 162
   travels to,
      California, 34, 43, 65, 83, 85
      New York, 34, 62, 67-68, 78
      Paris, 30, 31-32
      Texas, 119
      West and Midwest, 105, 108, 110, 158, 161
   views of,
      America, 115
      artists, 93
      beauty, 21

      critics, 119
      Hopper, Edward, 16, 62
      illness and mortality, 65, 83, 171, 176, 180
      landscapes, 81
      painting, 115-116
      photo-realism, 56
      politics, 56
      religion, 165
      upper class, 161
      West, 183
Register, John Sherman II, 175
Register, Karen Shumaker, 175, 176
Register, Kathryn, 36, 172, 175, 176, 180, 183
Register, Peter, 36, 89, 132, 161, 165, 168, 176, 180
Register, Samuel Croft, 25, 26
Register, Samuel Jr., 25, 26, 171
Reno, 119
Rest Area, 22
Restaurant by the Sea, 85, 88
   Study for, 89
Reventlow, Lance, 34
Rodin, Auguste, *The Thinker*, 105
Rooming House, 132, 136
Ross, Lillian, 105
Roth, William Matson, 56
Rourke, Mickey, 105
Ruscha, Ed, 161
San Francisco Chronicle, 62, 81
San Francisco Examiner, 38
San Francisco Museum of Modern Art, 30
Santa Ana Motor Parts, 60-61
Santa Barbara magazine, 75
San Jose Museum of Art, 179, 190
See Through, 171, 173
Seldis, Henry J., 52
Self-portrait, 40
Self-portrait, 171
Self-portrait on a Train, 115
Selz, Dr. Peter, 15-17
Sheeler, Charles, 16, 43
Sherman, Roger, 26
Sherman, Leila, 162
Shinn, James, 30
Sidon, Lex, 168
Sinclair, Upton, 32
Silver Lake, 101
Sketch for Prologue to 'Ask the Dust', 176
Spaeth, Eloise, 105
Southern Serves the South, 79
Southwest Motel, 85, 88
Soutine, Chaim, 97
Still Life with Lemons, 172
Stock, Mark, 81, 161
Storefront, 108
Studio Still Life, 172

Styron, William, 32
Suitcase, 185
Suits, 108, 109
Sunset magazine, 38
Swimmer, 132, 133
Te Amo, 85, 90-91
Texas Cafe, 130
Thiebaud, Wayne, 44
Three Tables, 156
Times Square, 137, 138-139
Train Compartment, 128
Train Interior, 115, 118
Twin Arrows Cafe, 166
Two Red Stools, 152
Two Telephones, 70, 165
   Study for, 70
Two Telephones, 1995, 165, 169
Uptown Downtown, 78
Uncle Wiggly Stories, The, 183
University of California, Berkeley, 30
Vacancy, 162, 163
Venetian Light, 12, 132
Ventura Freeway, 124
Vermeer, Jan, 48
View From the Train, 68, 74, 78
View of L.A., 27
View of Palm, 76, 77, 85
View of Venice Boardwalk, 8
Waiting at the Terminal (Airport), 132
Waiting Room, 68, 72 (and cover)
Waiting Room for the Beyond, 64, 81
Wall Phone, 21
Warhol, Andy, 44, 81
Wasteland Hotel, 120, 121, 132
Watching the Storm (Denver), 6-7, 115
West, Nathanael, 52
   Day of the Locust, 16
Westward Beach, 174
Wilde, Oscar, 31
William Sawyer Gallery, 62
Window of Opportunity, The, 135
   Study for, 134
Winona Motel, 137
Woman by the Sea, 165, 168
Wyeth, Andrew, 28, 28
Yellow Chair, 52, 53, 53
Yellow Couch, 73
Young & Rubicam, 36
Zeta Psi, 30